THE PARAS

50 YEARS OF COURAGE

FOREWORD

"The PARAS" is a tribute in words and pictures to the Men of the Airborne Forces and their first fifty years of devoted service to our Country.

It tells a story – many stories – of courage, of sacrifice and perhaps above all of loyalty to comrades.

From the earliest tentative beginnings and initial small-scale operations against the enemy we follow the birth of The Parachute Regiment and the growth of Airborne Forces, under the command of Lieutenant General Sir Frederick ("Boy") Browning, through the bitter fighting in North Africa and Sicily. through Normandy, Arnhem and the Rhine and the long chapter of post-war anti-terrorist operations.

This book shows clearly too how the Parachute Soldiers of today are upholding the great traditions they have inherited. It is particularly pleasing that The PARAS has come out during the Golden Jubilee of our Airborne Forces.

On behalf of all who have served in Airborne Forces I congratulate the Daily Star on their imaginative and welcome production of this tribute.

Major General JD Frost CB DSO MC DL
formerly Company Commander 2 PARA on the Bruneval Raid,
Commanding Officer 2 PARA in North Africa and at Arnhem,
GOC 52nd Lowland Division and latterly GOC Malta and Libya.

A Tribute to the Airborne Forces

HRH The Prince of Wales
KG KT GCB AK QSO PC ADC
Colonel-in-Chief
The Parachute Regiment

uthor David Reynolds in this book describes The Parachute Regiment as the Firefighters of the British Army. It is an appropriate description. For when there is a special job to be done, and urgently, that call most frequently comes to our Airborne Forces.

Airborne Forces are a young component of the British Army. It was on June 22, 1940 that Winston Churchill issued his historic directive to the Chiefs of Staff: "We ought to have a Corps of at least five thousand parachute troops . . ." Within three weeks the first parties of volunteers had assembled at Ringway – now Manchester Airport – and the training for war of Britain's first airborne forces had begun. These forces grew to include The Glider Pilot Regiment, selected battalions of famous Infantry regiments destined, with their supporting arms, to go into battle by glider, The Special Air Service Regiment and, formed within The Army Air Corps on August 1, 1942, The Parachute Regiment. Together with their colleagues in The Royal Air Force these units made very major contributions to victory in the Mediterranean theatre, in Europe and in the Far East. This book is published as a sincere tribute in this their Golden Jubilee Year to all units of our Airborne Forces and to All Ranks who have served in them in war or peace.

Despite being a newcomer to the Army's Order of Battle The Parachute Regiment has won a fine reputation with a list of Battle Honours extending from Bruneval in 1942 to the Falklands forty years later; and since 1945 parachute battalions have played consistently notable parts in the numerous and testing anti-terrorist operations in which the Army has been engaged from Palestine to Northern Ireland.

Today's Parachute Soldier in some ways bears little resemblance to his war-time predecessor. Gone is the Whitley bomber, the 'Pork Pie' helmet and the kit-bag carried on the drop. In have come parachutes with larger canopies, a reserve parachute and quite different weapons and methods of delivering them to the battlefield. And the radical advances in free-fall techniques now make possible the dropping of pathfinders and other specialists by day or night from great heights with full equipment.

Nevertheless the methods adopted in the early days of Airborne Forces for the selection, testing and training of the Parachute Soldier have remained fundamentally unchanged.

Moreover, despite all the advances in technology and technique the Parachute Soldier of today is in one vital respect identical to his Father or even his Grandfather: that is in the Regimental Spirit. Each man has the same sense of comradeship, the same loyalty to a team, sure in the knowledge that he can rely on his comrades just as they can rely on him.

Contents

AIRBORNE FORCES
1940–1990

Introduction

FIFTY YEARS OF AIRBORNE FORCES

Prime Minister Winston S Churchill

'We ought to have a Corps of at least 5,000
parachute troops. I hear something is being
done already to form such a Corps but only,
I believe, on a very small scale. Advantage
must be taken of the summer to train these
forces who can none the less play their part
meanwhile as shock troops in home defence.
Pray let me have a note from the War Office
on this subject.

**Minute from Prime Minister to Chiefs of Staff
22nd June 1940.**

BRITAIN'S Airborne Forces have served with distinction through fifty glorious years of service and established themselves as an elite fighting unit in the British Army.

The 'Red Beret' has a special significance to every man who has worn it, from the wartime units of the 1st and 6th Airborne divisions to the parachute soldiers of today.

Incorporating almost all of the specialist Corps, the tradesmen of the Army, the modern day airborne soldiers have become a household name and are better known as 'The Paras'.

They are Britain's 'fire brigade' shock troops of the 1990s trained in hostage rescue and on permanent standby to react to the unexpected anywhere in the world, in a tradition echoed by their regimental motto 'Ready for Anything'.

Since their creation by Winston Churchill in June 1940 the men of the Red Beret have been called on to carry out some of history's most difficult military operations – often destined to result in loss of life for the regiment. From Arnhem to Ulster the Paras have always been in the frontline of the action, winning 31 battle honours and hundreds of bravery decorations, including eight Victoria Crosses.

During World War Two Britain's airborne forces totalled more than 40,000 men and included 17 parachute battalions, many of whom were drawn from county regiments such as the Royal Hampshires, the Royal Welch Fusiliers and the Green Howards.

Other units called up for parachute training included the Kings Regt, the Royal Sussex, the South Staffordshire Regt, the Cameron Highlanders and the Somerset Light Infantry.

The glider borne battalions, which played a vital role during World War Two, were drawn from the Border Regt, the Royal Ulster Rifles, the Black Watch, the Argyll and Sutherland Highlanders, the Devonshire Regt, the Oxfordshire and Buckinghamshire Light Infantry and the Kings Own Scottish Borderers.

Both parachute battalions and glider trained units included the support of individual skills from the Royal Artillery, the Royal Armoured Corps, the Royal Engineers, the Royal Army Medical Corps, the Royal Signals and the Royal Army Service Corps, all of whom wore the Red Beret.

The Polish Parachute Brigade, the Canadian Parachute Battalion and the Indian Parachute Brigade joined together to form one huge 'airborne family'.

It was in a memo to the War Office that the wartime Prime Minister instructed chiefs of staff to form 'a corps of at least 5,000 parachute troops' as a means of striking back at the Germans, who were already using parachute trained troops, and threatened to invade Britain.

This new force was officially formed on

Left: The Red Berets march past at Rushmoor arena in Aldershot to mark the Golden anniversary of Airborne Forces.

Below, far left: Volunteers for airborne service pictured during physical training tests in September 1942.

Below left: A Para, wearing the helmet and equipment used during the 1970s, protects the 'drop zone' as his colleagues land in an exercise jump.

Below: Gunners of the 7th Para Regiment Royal Horse Artillery fire their Howitzers during range tests.

Left: Survivors of the raid on Bruneval meet with serving Paras to mark the 40th anniversary of Operation Biting. The group includes General John Frost and Lt. Col. 'H' Jones, who was killed in the Falklands.
Below: Wearing his Red Beret General Frost CBE, DSO, MC, the man who commanded 2 Para at Arnhem Bridge returns to remember fallen colleagues.
Opposite page: A Para armed with an M16, Armalite, on patrol in the 'bandit countryside' of south Armagh, Northern Ireland.

June 22, 1940, and the first volunteers for 'special service' began their parachute training several weeks later at Ringway in Manchester. The first jump was recorded on July 13.

The volunteers joined up with men of No. 2 Commando to be renamed the 11th Special Air Service Battalion and by the end of 1940 were 500 strong. They were both parachute and glider trained.

Today soldiers jump from RAF C-130 Hercules aircraft, but in 1940 the pioneers of military parachuting who volunteered for 'special service' found themselves dropping from a hole in the floor of a Whitley bomber, often hitting their faces on the way out in what became known as the 'Whitley kiss'.

In 1941 the success of the first airborne operation signalled the way ahead for the future of Britain's parachute trained troops when just 38 men dropped into southern Italy and destroyed the Tragino Aqueduct.

That was followed by a daring raid into France, led by Major John Frost of 2 Para, to dismantle a German radar dish and bring it back to England for scientists to examine.

General Frost CBE, DSO, MC and Bar, has since become a legend within the Parachute regiment after going on to serve in North Africa and command 2 Para at Arnhem when he and his men held the vital road bridge until they ran out of ammunition. He believes the shared fear of jumping into battle is what makes the Paras a special force forming an invisible bond of comradeship that can only be understood by those who have experienced it.

By the end of 1942 the 1st Airborne

Above: The commander of British Airborne Forces, Major General Federick 'Boy' Browning. *Right:* General Montgomery presents the DSO to Colonel Parker, whose initial unit was the Green Howards.

Division had been formed and General Frederick 'Boy' Browning was appointed commanding officer of the new force, which included the Glider Pilot Regiment and Army Air Corps, both established on December 21, 1941.

Determined to make his men stand out as a unique and proud force, General Browning adopted the maroon beret for airborne troops as a hallmark to be remembered by others, especially the enemy. He is believed to have taken the idea after reading a novel by his wife, Daphne du Maurier, in which the leading character wore a red beret to attract attention. After much deliberation with senior colleagues over the colour and possibility that blue would be better, he asked his orderly to decide and the red beret became the elite head dress of airborne units.

In August 1942 the Parachute Regiment was given its now famous name, but although soldiers wore the red beret they continued to wear the cap badge of their own regiment until later in 1943 when their own was minted.

They went on to win their spurs at a host of savage wartime battles and fifty years later are respected and feared by soldiers and terrorists throughout the world, after a history of always completing an operation – whatever the cost.

In 1941 they dropped into battle in North Africa from just 500ft, half today's training limit, and despite being heavily outnumbered by the Germans, they refused to surrender – in one battle they lost 250 men and 16 officers.

The Germans were so fearful of the Paras determination to win at whatever cost, they nicknamed them the 'Red Devils', a name which stuck and was later adopted as the name for the regiment's freefall display team.

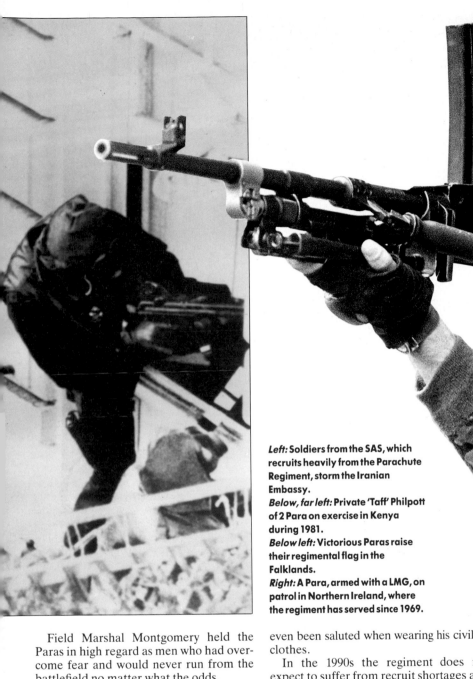

Left: **Soldiers from the SAS, which recruits heavily from the Parachute Regiment, storm the Iranian Embassy.**
Below, far left: **Private 'Taff' Philpott of 2 Para on exercise in Kenya during 1981.**
Below left: **Victorious Paras raise their regimental flag in the Falklands.**
Right: **A Para, armed with a LMG, on patrol in Northern Ireland, where the regiment has served since 1969.**

Field Marshal Montgomery held the Paras in high regard as men who had overcome fear and would never run from the battlefield no matter what the odds.

After Arnhem he told the war cabinet: 'They have jumped from the air and by doing so have conquered fear. They are proud of their honour and have never failed in any task. They are in fact, men apart. Every man an Emperor.'

That view is supported by a senior officer who transferred to the Paras and found that paratroopers refused to salute him within the walls of their own camp, although would respect his commission outside.

'It soon became clear that these guys would follow their officers anywhere, but they made their disgust for non-parachute trained officers very clear, and politely attempted to avoid saluting me – until I had my wings up.'

Later, that same man became one of the regiment's most respected officers and has even been saluted when wearing his civilian clothes.

In the 1990s the regiment does not expect to suffer from recruit shortages as it has a constant list of young men applying to join the crack unit and pass its tough selection course.

It is a physically demanding programme of severe physical tests, which each potential paratrooper must pass before he can commence his parachute training. From the minute they arrive at the depot they must race to every lecture, rise at the crack of dawn and be prepared for 'call-outs' in the middle of the night – all designed to test each man to his limit.

In the final selection recruits must be able to 'tab' a combination of running and walking, carrying 45lbs over a distance of 10 miles in just 1 hour and 45 minutes – faster

Above: **Combat Royal Engineers of 9 Para Squadron seated inside an RAF C-130 Hercules wait for the doors to open, and left, the Green Light to jump.**
Right: **Para serving with 5 Airborne Brigade prepares to jump from an RAF Chinook helicopter at Hankley common 'drop zone' near Aldershot.**

than any other regiment in the British Army, excluding the SAS.

The 26-week course is regarded as one of the toughest challenges in the world and is based totally on speed; a point which is brought home to rookies in the early stages of their arrival at the depot. The commanding officer of recruit training, Lt Col Donald Campbell, says 'It is without doubt a physically demanding course, but people must realise that these men are not supermen. Any man can become a paratrooper if he has the determination and qualities to succeed'.

The man who will lead the Paras into the 1990s, Regimental Colonel Hamish McGregor, MC, believes his men are the finest in the world – 'their skills, flexibility and sheer professionalism, make them a force very much in demand. These young men face the toughest course in the world, excluding the SAS, and they are truly the most professional soldiers'.

Proud of their coveted beret, the Paras do not wear a dress cap like other regiments, instead they wear their beret at all times whether in battle or marching before the Queen. It is a distinction which only they can boast.

Above the recruit's store at Aldershot a sign hangs bearing the words 'No pain, No gain' to warn potential Paras of the gruelling demands that lie ahead of them in their bid to earn the red beret and parachute wings. But the phrase is also a true reflection of what is to be expected of a Para in battle and time and time again generations of young men have demonstrated the fighting tradition of the regiment – never give in.

At Arnhem Bridge, Frost and his men refused to surrender and suffered the pain of heavy casualties. In the Falklands, 2 Para faced an awesome task at Goose Green, but battled through to win. *Today, des-

pite being the youngest operational regiment in the British Army, the Paras have already joined the ranks of the Chelsea Pensioners, with Sergeant Jack Turner and Sergeant Major Jim Priestly recording another first for the regiment – this time, as part of history. Sergeant Turner, General Frost's wartime driver, and para medic Sgt Maj Priestly, both proudly wear the coveted parachute wings on their Chelsea Pensioners' tunic.

The Golden Jubilee of Airborne Forces was celebrated by the Paras on June 22, 1990, when with bayonets fixed the regiment marched through the streets of London –

exactly 50 years after Winston Churchill had created them.

More than 3,500 past and present soldiers of airborne units joined the birthday honour in a thanksgiving service at St Paul's Cathedral to pay tribute to their airborne comrades.

Wearing full uniform and wings, which he earned by completing the course in 1977, Prince Charles took the salute as General John Graham headed a march past of veterans, which included Sir Anthony Farrar Hockley and Maj Gen John Frost.

Now as airborne forces look forward to the next 50 years, the Paras have been

selected to head a special 'out of area' force trained to deal with hostilities and the protected evacuation of UK nationals, outside the Nato environment.

Called 5 Airborne Brigade, the new unit, formed in 1983, currently incorporates two parachute battalions and a wide range of specialists to provide medical, signal and engineer support in a format first adopted by the wartime founders of the 1st and 6th Airborne Divisions.

Ulster Defence regiment was formed in 1969, but does not operate outside Northern Ireland as an operational unit.

SOLDIERS OF THE RED BERET

The airborne infantrymen of the British Army, the Paras unique role has demanded, since their creation, that equipment and uniform be tailored to suit their needs.

Today, as during the early days, the physical aspect of training is based on a combination of stamina and speed. The two are vital to the Paratrooper in getting away from the drop zone as quickly as possible, often carrying more than 100lbs on his back.

Arnhem 1944

Our Para is wearing the standard battle dress of airborne troops who fought at Arnhem in 1944. His Red Beret, introduced by General Frederick 'Boy' Browning, bears the metal cap badge of the Parachute Regiment, issued in late 1943.

Prior to this, parachute trained soldiers wore the Red Beret with the cap badge of their former regiment before they volunteered for 'special service'.

His Denison smock jacket was specially designed for airborne soldiers and first issued in 1942. Its baggy shape allowed troops to stow their parachute packing bag inside it during the jump.

Early versions had a half-length zip, storm cuffs and button-fastening tabs at the front. Many soldiers sewed the tops of their woollen socks to the cuffs to make them windproof. The style of this jacket proved so popular that it is still in use today, albeit in a modified form.

Around his neck the wartime Para wears a face veil which was, and still is, used for camouflage and concealment. His webbing is of the 1937 pattern, clearly showing two ammunition

pouches worn at the front.

They were packed full of extra ammunition for his 9mm Sten machine gun Mk II, frequently used by airborne troops, whose requirements influenced its design.

Note the rope toggle, carried around the neck and secured to the soldiers belt. It was a versatile item of equipment which used in conjunction with other toggles improvised to help Paras scale walls and other difficult obstacles.

Trousers were heavy and made of rough serge material with a special chamois-lined pocket on the left leg for maps and a right thigh 'knife' pocket. The battle dress trousers were known as BD.

Ankle high boots with steel toecaps and studs in the sole were heavy but robust and officially titled 'ammunition boots'. They were supported by canvas anklets, secured around the leg by two fasteners.

ILLUSTRATION BY GARY COOK

Para of 1990

Our Para of 1990 is wearing the same style of clothing as his wartime colleague, although today's uniform is lighter and more efficient after years of development.

His Denison smock is windproof and made from a light camouflage cloth known as **DPM (Disruptive Pattern Material)**. Today the elasticated cuffs are standard and as well as a full-length zip a small pocket has been added to the left sleeve for a field dressing.

He is wearing '58 pattern webbing, which after a successful service with the British Army is due to be replaced with a system called **PLCE (Personal Load Carrying Equipment)**.

A **DZ** flash indicating which battalion he is serving with is worn on the right arm just below his parachute wings, set exactly two fingers depth below the top of the sleeve.

The modern-day Para carries the hi-tech SA80 weapon, which was introduced in the mid '80s to replace the larger SLR (Self Loading Rifle). Smaller, but more accurate than its predecessor, the new rifle has a special sight built into it.

Trousers are also windproof and made from a lightweight camouflage material, which allows them to dry quicker if the soldier is soaked during training.

Today's boots are the ultimate design. Again they are lightweight and have a special sole which is moulded directly to the boot. Variations of this 'high combat' boot are constantly being updated.

1990 Wings and wartime insignia.

Above and *right:* Pioneers on the Vickers 'Vimy. The first users of parachutes were professional stunt men who climbed onto the wings of an aircraft and while holding on to the strut of the fuselage pulled their own rip cord, deploying the canopy into the slipstream which pulled the parachutist off. This was the 'pull-off' method.

Chapter one

THE SPIRIT OF PARACHUTING

THE AIRCRAFT echoes a silent confidence as the Paras patiently wait for the doors to open, blasting in fresh air and signalling that the drop is close. Luxuries are sparse, they sit packed tightly in four rows wearing their parachutes and carrying more than 100lbs of equipment; there are no windows and the stewardess is a burly RAF jump instructor. The atmosphere inside the camouflaged transporter is claustrophobic and silent, the air is choked by engine fumes and every Para has just one thing on his mind – to get out of the aircraft as soon as possible.

These men of 1 Para are sat aboard the workhorse of today's airborne forces, a C-130 Hercules of the RAF's 47 squadron based at Lyneham in Wiltshire, and can often spend as long as 4 hours flying to a drop zone. The Hercules can carry 90 fully equipped Paras who are divided into jumping groups called 'sticks'. At 'P' hour, parachute hour, these sticks will exit from both port and starboard doors in a system called 'simsticks'.

As the adrenalin starts to pump around the body, hands begin to sweat with anxiety and pre-jump nerves. But as soon as they are brought to action the butterflies disappear and each man's training takes over in a calm professional manner.

The aircraft's seats are packed away, they hook up and their static lines given a final safety check as the RAF parachute instructors open the doors ready to despatch their sticks. The Number One stands rigid in the door watching a set of lights to his left and listening to the command of the jump

Left: Paratroopers in their old-style rubber helmets and baggy smocks carrying a container packed with all the heavy equipment and weapons they cannot jump with. These containers were fixed underneath the plane and dropped separately. *Above:* Women of the WAAF performing the vital task of packing parachutes. *Below:* Waiting to ride 'the elephant', as the Whitley bomber was known.

master. It flashes red then green as the command GO is shouted and the stream of paratroopers pours out into the open skies.

The four-week course includes two jumps from a balloon, five from an aircraft during daylight and one at night. There is no room for half measures, you either jump or you fail and those who tell you they are not frightened on their first drop are lying.

After numerous safety checks, lectures and procedures, the promising Para students are rigged for their first jump . . . from a balloon basket 800ft above Weston on the Green in Oxfordshire.

Only four jumpers at a time take to the skies, the silence is eerie and the cage swings about in the wind. For many this form of jumping is worse than leaping from a plane. There is no slipstream and the student drops like a stone, falling 200ft before his parachute fully deploys.

One veteran RAF instructor summed up the balloon jump: 'It's the nearest thing I can imagine to suicide, it's like jumping off a bridge. But it's the second jump that often cracks them, they know what to expect and think about it too much'.

Sat in the aircraft every rookie jumper tries to hide his fear of hearing the door open for the first jump from a Hercules, double-checking all the drills taught to him as the 'tell off equipment check' order is made minutes before streaming out.

Seconds later every man is out in the skies overjoyed at seeing his canopy fully deployed above him and preparing himself to land, his fear passed . . . for the time being.

Modern day equipment is among the best in the world and the training procedures tried and tested by the RAF's No. 1 Parachute Training School have been adopted by many other forces. But the pioneers of British military parachuting carried no reserves, had no experience to learn from and no special aircraft to jump from. Instead they dropped through the disused mid-under turret in the floor of Whitley bombers.

In 1797 Andre-Jacques Garnerin made the first ever successful parachute descent and by 1925 the Italians had established a military parachuting school, closely followed by the French, Polish and American armies. Russia also entered the airborne field, but it was the Germans who became the architects of military jumping using the parachute troops to punch their advance across Europe and threaten an invasion of Britain.

After the war office had acted on Prime Minister Churchill's instruction to form a corps of 5,000 parachute troops, Ringway airport at Manchester was selected as the base for airborne training under the banner of the Central Landing Establishment.

During the First World War, British military personnel manning observation balloons were given parachutes as a chance of survival if attacked, but the only real use of parachutes had been by professional stuntmen. They climbed onto the wing of an aircraft and while holding onto the strut of the fuselage pulled their own rip cord, deploying the canopy into the slipstream which pulled the parachutist off. This style was known as the 'pull-off' method and required extreme courage by the jumper.

It was this dare-devil procedure that was first adopted by the military at Ringway and adapted in a jumping procedure from a Whitley bomber over the training school's Tatton Park drop zone. The parachutist had to crawl through the fuselage to the rear gunner's turret which had been removed. Then standing on a tiny platform with the aircraft's rudders either side of him, totally exposed to the slipstream, he was ordered to pull his ripcord.

It was according to those who made 'pull-off' jumps, a frightening experience and the alternative exit through a hole in the floor of a Whitley bomber was favoured, although the original style of jumping was maintained for some time to introduce men to parachuting.

The first troops at RAF Ringway, from No. 2 Commando, had to complete five jumps to get their wings. However, training was suddenly halted when the parachute of driver Evans failed to open.

His colleagues watched helplessly as he plunged to the ground in a horrific death, an accident which was to happen again and

became known as a 'Roman Candle'. It was, and still is, the greatest fear of every Para. After extensive checks to the parachute design and modifications to the harness, training resumed; but Evans wasn't to be the last casualty, by the end of 1940, at least three men had died.

As the demand for parachute-trained troops increased, activity at Ringway soared and more than 2,000 descents were recorded by the end of 1940. The qualified

soldiers of No. 2 Commando were then renamed the 11th Special Air Service Battalion.

A whole new range of military equipment was developed to meet the needs of the airborne soldier, including a special rubber helmet, later to be replaced with a steel model, and a baggy smock which is still in service today, albeit in a modified form. A folding mini-motorcycle was introduced and dropped onto the DZ in an

Taking to the skies on a practice jump *(above)*. The first man leaps when over the target area — the white T-Shape clearly visible in the photo. Paratroopers are trained so that they can make an almost vertical fall by pulling the front or rear 'lift-webs' of their parachutes. Attached to the parachute pack on his back is a static-line fastened to the plane. When this line snaps tight as he falls, the cover of the parachute is ripped out, air gets under the first folds of the parachute and quickly drags it out of the container.

Training in the early days at Ringway *(far left)*. Waiting to be 'pushed away' for a controlled jump from the parachute tower — September 1942.

Left: Paratroopers in their 'pork-pies' (rubber helmets), enjoying a swift cuppa in front of a YMCA tea van during a break in training.

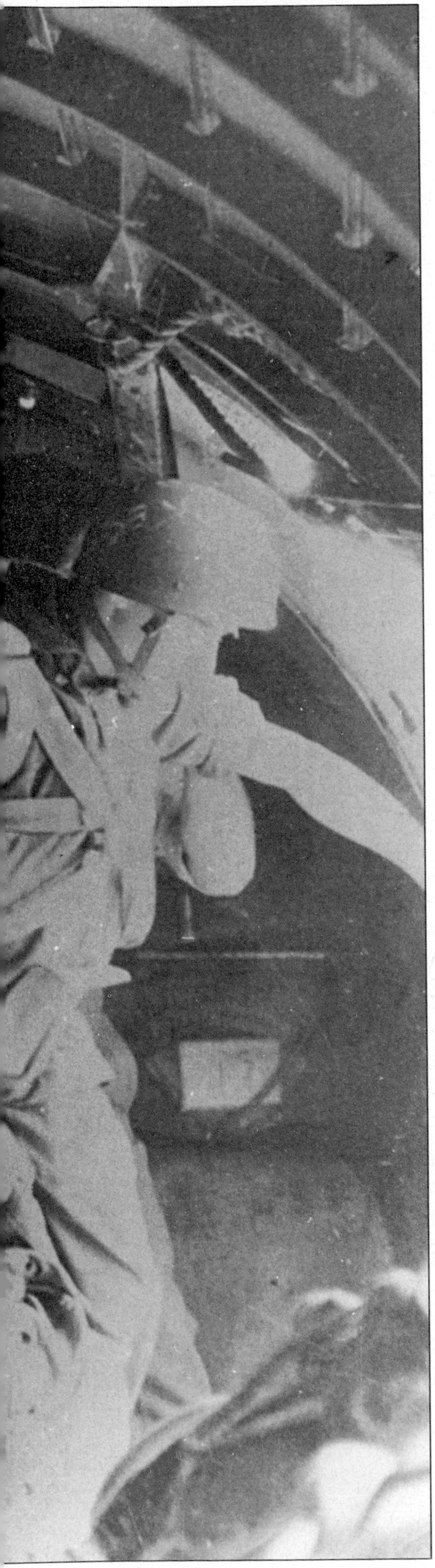

equipment container along with a bicycle which could be packed away in sections.

The packing of each parachute was a precision job and in the main carried out by women of the Women's Auxiliary Air Force. The job was very demanding and needed maximum concentration – a person's life depended on it.

Members of the WAAF also manned the ambulances at Tatton Park DZ and provided a 'listening ear' at the tea trucks for the newly arrived rookies fearful of their first jump. In the words of one Para, 'they kept us going with words of encouragement and packed our parachutes with sheer dedication, they were part of the team'.

By 1942, the war-weary Paras had the luxury of jumping from the American Dakotas, complete with windows and one side door, making despatching quicker and less fraught than dropping through the 'hell hole' of a Whitley.

At Arnhem in 1944 a 10,000-strong force of parachute and glider troops rained down from the skies to make an airborne assault on German forces in a battle that was to become a legend in military history, despite its failure to conquer the enemy.

Following the war years, military free-fall parachuting was born at Abingdon and the specialist work of training the SAS in high altitude low level, HALO, techniques began, along with the introduction of the Hercules.

Today the role of Britain's Paras requires them to jump from helicopters as well as aircraft and all parachute training is still carried out by RAF instructors who preach their motto to all new students – 'Knowledge Dispels Fear'.

The door opens, blasting in fresh air and signalling that the drop is close. Within minutes the stick will be on the ground. *Left:* Paratroopers waiting for the jump. 'Go!' A body hurtles into space *(below)*. This paratrooper is carrying an automatic weapon ready for instant action when he touches down.

Travelling in style on the
Whitley bomber.
Despatch from these
planes was through the
aperture in the floor.

Chapter two

FIRST AIRBORNE OPERATIONS

Left: Paratroopers and landing craft. Below: Aerial map of the raid on Bruneval, which took place in February 1942.

THE RAID ON BRUNEVAL

BRITAIN'S first airborne assault took place in 1941, when the Paras introduced themselves to the enemy by jumping into Italy and blowing up an aqueduct in a daring raid named Operation Colossus.

Water from the Tragino aqueduct was pumped by pipeline to supply Italian forces and was the perfect target to gain maximum propaganda, destroying the enemy's morale. But it was too far inland for a sea-borne raid and too difficult to bomb. An airborne assault was the obvious answer and it was the opportunity Whitehall Chiefs had been seeking to test Churchill's new force, which was only seven months old.

In total 38 men of what was then called the 11th Special Air Service battalion dropped from two Whitley bombers, having had just three weeks of training, in which one man, L/Sgt Dennis, was killed when he landed in a lake and drowned.

Codenamed Operation Colossus, the raid took place on the night of February 10, 1941, and it was intended that after blowing up the aqueduct, the unit would make their way to the coast to be picked up by the submarine HMS Triumph.

The objective was destroyed, but the entire force was captured as they headed for the rendezvous with the senior service. It later transpired that one of the Whitley planes which had dropped the men, had crashed near the spot where the Triumph was due to surface and had been diverted away after enemy warships searched for the plane's aircrew.

It was almost a year later that the regiment was called on to carry out a daring 'behind the lines' raid, of vital importance to the war office. The operation was so successful that it attracted applause from Prime Minister Winston Churchill and guaranteed the Paras wartime future.

The aim of Operation Biting was to dismantle a Wurzburg precision radar dish, which was one of a series of early warning installations on the north coast of France, and bring it back to England for scientific research.

Admiral Lord Mountbatten had proposed the raid, after it became clear that this established chain of radar stations was of significant importance to the Luftwaffe, who were inflicting heavy losses on RAF Bomber command. But the radar posts were heavily defended against attack from the sea with machine guns looking down onto the beach and hidden barbed wire surrounding the radars. It was a task only airborne troops could accomplish.

Paras who took part in the Bruneval raid
chat to Sqd. Ldr. Pickard, the RAF pilot
who dropped them for the raid. *Left:* Paras
climb aboard a landing craft during training
for Bruneval.

When the RAF brought back pictures of a radar system near Le Havre, situated high on an isolated clifftop near the village of Bruneval, the Chief of Combined Operations agreed to mount a recovery raid aimed at bringing elements of the dish back to the UK for research.

The task was given to Major John Frost and his men of C Company (Charlie) 2 Para, otherwise known within the brigade as 'Jock' company, for its obvious high contingent of troops from Scottish regiments. They were to be dropped into France in three separate groups and carry out their mission with the support of an RAF radar expert and then be picked up by a mini flotilla of six Royal Navy landing craft.

In recognition of the joint operation with the Admiralty, each group of 40 paras was named after a famous sailor, 'Nelson', 'Drake', and 'Rodney' – a gesture to the senior service which was never forgotten by the Navy.

On the night of February 27, 1942, the 120-strong force took off from Thruxton Aerodrome in a fleet of 12 Whitley bombers, each carrying 10 men, and jumped in perfect weather conditions into France.

The operation met strong resistance, three men were killed and a further seven badly injured. But it had been a total success, the vital equipment secured and a German radar expert captured.

Of these first airborne operations perhaps the least known is Operation Freshman, which involved glider borne troops of the Royal Engineers in November 1942.

In this, the first glider assault, airborne troops were tasked to land in northern Norway and destroy the Norsk Hydro plant. The objective, near the village of Rjuken, was set in difficult terrain for any form of assault. The village was situated in a deep valley banking and surrounded by thick forest, which banked almost vertically 3,000 ft from the river bed.

Sat 1,000 ft above the river was the heavy water plant, an impossible target for bombers. After extensive preparation the tiny force took off from Scotland in two gliders towed by RAF bombers. The weather however, was bad and both gliders sustained heavy landings killing many of the 34 sappers. Those remaining were captured and interrogated by the Gestapo.

The men who had taken part in the operation were all volunteers from the 9th Field Company (Airborne) RE and the 261st Field Park Company (Airborne) RE, specialists in demolition.

Later when the war had finished the 1st Airborne division arrived in Norway and the fate of the engineers was revealed – all survivors of the landings had been executed.

Glider troops (1st Airborne Division), North Africa 1943, beside a US (WACO) glider, one of many used for airlifting troops to Sicily.

Chapter three
NORTH AFRICA SICILY AND ITALY

THE maroon beret was first seen by German troops in north Africa and within months they had christened the ferocious Paras *Rote Teufel* – Red Devils.

This distinctive head dress, since adopted by parachute troops all over the world, was officially introduced in 1942, at the direction of General Browning, and the Pegasus symbol – Bellerophon astride winged Pegasus – became the emblem of British Airborne Forces.

Allied forces had invaded Algeria and Morocco on November 8, in an operation which was planned to cut off German supply routes from Europe. Days later 3 Para made the first operational battalion drop in a successful assault at Bone airfield, on November 12.

The 1st Parachute Brigade, comprising three battalions and supporting elements, were sent to north Africa by sea – except the 3rd battalion, who had been airlifted for the Bone assault from St Eval in Cornwall, travelling via Gibraltar.

Later when the Paras captured a group of 200 Germans in February 1943, they discovered they were carrying special instructions, telling how best to fight the *Rote Teufel*. They were overjoyed at the respect they had gained from the Germans. General Haig congratulated them and General Browning sent a message saying 'Such distinctions are seldom given in war and then only to the finest fighting troops'.

The Dakota *(right)* **as used in operations in Africa, Italy and Sicily.** *Below:* **1st Parachute Brigade, North Africa 1943.** *Below right:* **A German plane shot down by bren gun fire.**

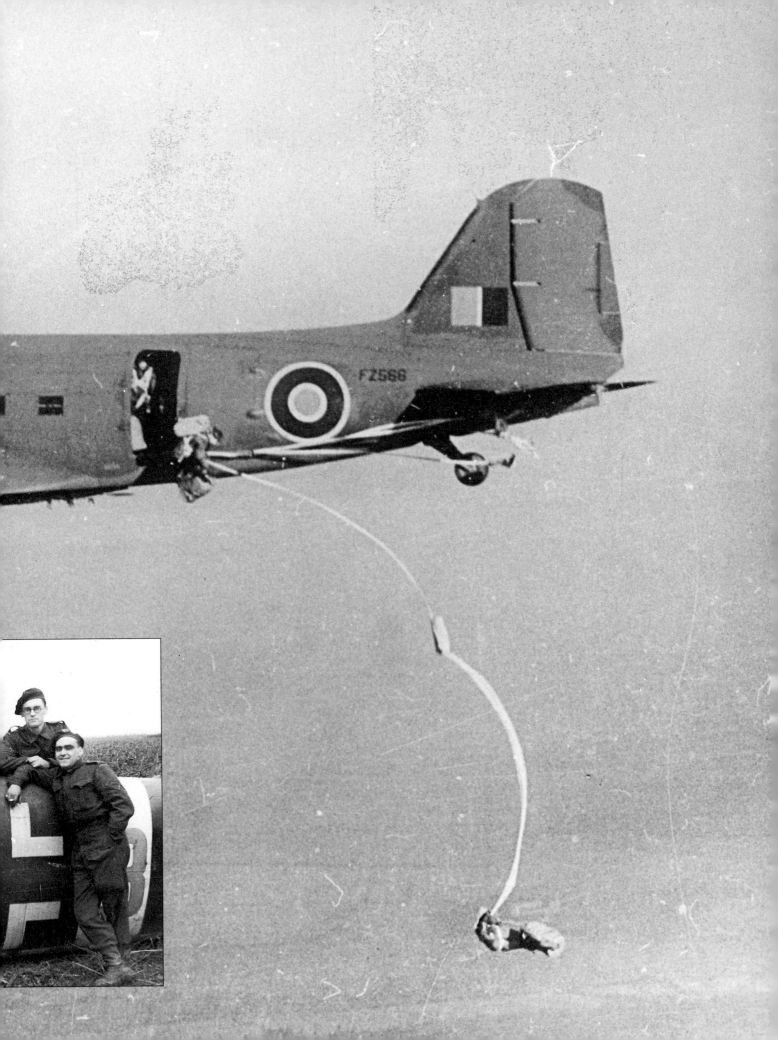

In November 1942, Frost, who now commanded 2 Para was tasked to mount an operation against enemy held airfields near Depienne, 30 miles south of Tunis.

The battalion dropped, but found the airfield was abandoned and a column of armour scheduled to meet up with 2 Para at Oudna never arrived, leaving them abandoned 50 miles behind enemy lines.

They were soon attacked and heavily outnumbered by German units, but fought like lions to battle their way back to Allied lines in a series of ambushes and fire fights, which cost the lives of 16 officers and 250 men.

Unknown to Frost, history would repeat itself just a couple of years later, when 2 Para would find themselves cut off again at Arnhem bridge and again, he would be in command.

Veteran Para, Harry Tucker, who served with 1 Para, remembers arriving in north Africa and getting a mixed reception from Senior Army officers – 'When we first arrived, the Army brass didn't have a lot of time for us, because we were a new regiment with no history. But we soon proved ourselves, we fought all the way from Algiers to Tunis'.

Later Cpl Tucker, now 73, was shot by a sniper and wounded by a grenade blast within days of jumping into Arnhem.

By 1943, the 1st Parachute Brigade had taken part in more battles than any other

Right: **The Civil War in Greece, December 1944. British troops have been given the task of clearing the city of Athens of all ELAS troops. A typical job allotted to them was the 'winkling' out of ELAS troops from the EAM building. A tank charged the door with machine guns blazing, and then the paratroopers entered. Some 30 prisoners were taken, some of them women. Previously, British troops had been unable to use their firearms, and had consequently suffered many embarrassments. Here, paratroopers take up a position behind cover on a street corner. Heavy fighting continued until Jan. 1945.** *Below:* **An airborne sniper waits for ELAS to vacate a burning building – Athens, 1944.**

formation in the 1st Army, capturing 3,000 prisoners and inflicting more than 5,000 casualties on the enemy, with the loss of 1,700 of its own men.

In February the Brigade had taken up a position on the right of the Allied line and found itself facing a force of Germans in divisional strength, determined to break through the British formation. But despite facing constant artillery attacks, the Paras succeeded in holding the line, in weather conditions more reminiscent of Salisbury plain than north Africa.

In June 1943, the 2nd and 4th Parachute Brigades, as well as the 1st Air Landing Brigade, had joined the depleted 1st Brigade in north Africa to comprise the 1st Airborne Division, as preparations were made for further operations, into Italy and Sicily.

The capture of Sicily was planned as a quick pincer attack with the Americans advancing from the west and the British 8th Army from the east. Airborne troops were to capture key bridges and ports ahead of the main force, preventing the enemy escaping into Italy across the Messina gap.

The seaborne landings were set for July 10, and to assist the beach assault, the 1st Air Landing Brigade was ordered to capture Porté Grande on the evening of July 9.

Above: Two Paras search a civilian suspect in front of a wall daubed with KKE graffiti, Dec., 1944. *Right:* A soldier of the 2nd Parachute Battalion stands at a memorial in the 'Red River Valley' (Tamara Valley).

More than 2,000 airborne troops embarked aboard a fleet of Horsa gliders in north Africa and were towed by RAF bombers to their objectives in Sicily. But the weather was severe and many of the gliders crashed while others were shot down by friend and foe before they had even reached the coast.

The 1st Air Landing captured the Ponte Grande, which ensured an almost unopposed landing for the beach forces, before the Germans began a counter attack against the lightly-equipped airborne troops. The 8th Army soon swept through Ponte Grande to support the 1st Air Landing Brigade and regained control as they pushed inland and north towards Catania and Messina.

Catania was a vital base line for the final advance on Messina and the 1st Parachute Brigade was ordered to take a bridge where the main road crossed the river, called the Ponte di Primosole.

On July 13, more than 112 aircraft and 16 gliders carrying 1,856 men, took off from north Africa. Their initial target was to capture the Primosole bridge and the high ground around it, providing a pathway for the 8th Army, but heavy anti-aircraft fire shot down many of the Dakotas before sticks could even jump out. Only 295 officers and men were dropped close enough to carry out the assault on the bridge.

The German 4th Parachute Brigade counter attacked and after a fierce battle, the tiny force of airborne troops withdrew to a second line and continued firing, but the bridge was back in enemy hands.

After the arrival of the 8th Army, the bridge was recaptured by the 9th Battalion the Durham Light Infantry, being guided by Lt Col Alistair Pearson of 1 Para and the remnants of the Brigade.

Fighting in Sicily ended on August 17, 1943, and in September the 1st Airborne Division was sent to capture the port of Taranto in Italy by means of a seaborne assault.

On August 15, 1944, parachute units, which included the 4th, 5th and 6th Para battalions and 1st Ind Pathfinders, dropped between Frejus and Cannes. Their objective was to capture the area, destroy all enemy positions and hold the ground until the American Seventh Army came ashore. The drop was almost unopposed and within days the British parachute group was withdrawn by sea to Italy in readiness for future operations.

on October 12, 1944, the same parachute formation was tasked to capture the airfield at Megara, 30 miles west of Athens, and restore the legally elected Government from communist inspired forces.

Bad weather hit the operation and when one company of 4 Para jumped on Megara airfield in wind speeds of 35mph, they suffered 50 per cent casualties. Constant high winds prevented the remainder of the force from jumping until the following day.

For the next three months, the Brigade was busy following up the withdrawal of German forces and restoring law and order. The most important task in Operation Manna lay in Athens.

Conditions there had deteriorated rapidly between the Government forces and communist backed political groups of the KKE and ELAS, which resulted in heavy street fighting constantly involving the Paras. This continued until January 1945, when the rebels were finally defeated and the brigade was withdrawn to Italy in February 1945.

While the 1st Airborne Division had been operating in north Africa and Europe, the Indian Army had created its own airborne forces. On October 18, 1941 the 151st Para Battalion was formed from soldiers serving in the Indian Army.

Later this unit was joined by the 152nd (Indian) and 153rd (Gurkha) Para Bns.

Chapter four
THE NORMANDY INVASION

D-Day + 1. Air Landing Brigade. British airborne troops led the D-Day landings in a combined parachute and glider assault to protect the eastern flank of the Allied bridgehead in Normandy.

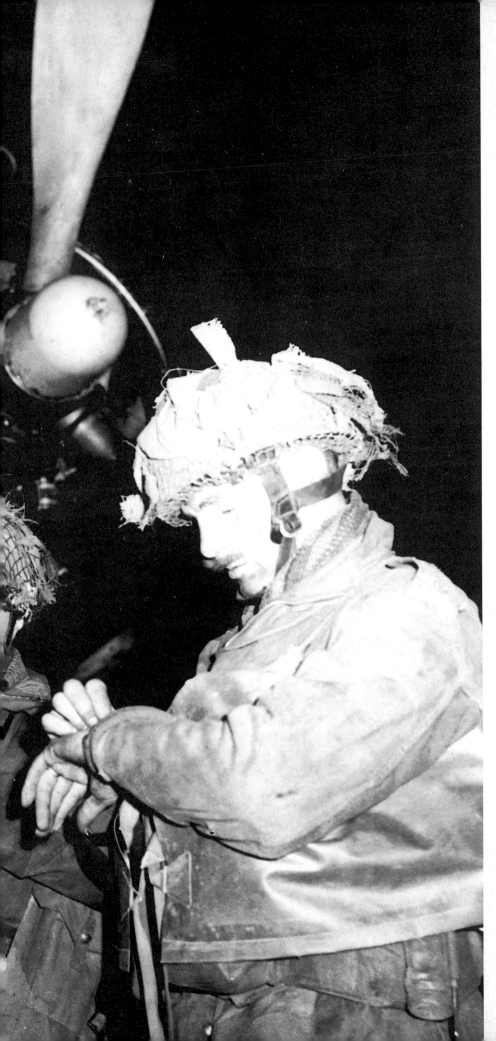

AIRBORNE troops led the D-Day landings in a combined parachute and glider assault, to throw a net of protection around the Normandy beaches, where a massive invasion force would sweep ashore and advance into Europe.

Among their initial objectives, the British airborne units were to destroy a German gun battery which threatened the lives of seaborne troops, and protect the left flank of the sea assault by seizing strategic points, which would prevent the enemy from reaching the beaches.

Preparations had been going on for three years prior to the invasion of Normandy, with new roles being created and units formed, including the 6th Airborne Division on May 18, 1943. The number 'six' being chosen to hoodwink the enemy and fool them into believing that Britain already had five airborne divisions, when in fact it had just two, the 1st and 6th, under General Browning.

Operation Overlord 'D-Day' on June 6, 1944, involved the massed troops of two Allied armies pouring into France to drive the Germans out of the country, after the 6th Airborne division had dropped and captured key points, including a heavily fortified gun battery.

The division, which had been born in 1943, was under the command of General Gale, and included glider and parachute troops from many different regiments, all wearing the distinctive red beret of airborne forces.

There were now ten glider squadrons operating under the control of No. 38 group RAF, and today, at the end of the old runway at Harwell, now the Atomic Research Establishment, a memorial marks the spot where the first gliders left for D-Day.

Bad weather had delayed the invasion by 24 hours, but late on the night of June 5, the force of Dakotas and Horsa gliders towed by RAF bombers took off for the invasion of Normandy.

First in were the pathfinders of 22nd Independent Parachute company, with Lt De La Tour being the first man on the ground. They were tasked to mark the drop zone and guide the parachute and glider units in using special Eureka beacons.

Few were dropped accurately, as the Germans had flooded the low-lying ground around the Orne and Dives rivers, destroying many identifying features which had been given to pilots as 'markers' during the intense pre-flight brief.

Unit planning had been very detailed, especially by the 9 Para, who had been tasked to silence the Merville gun battery

***Left:* The airborne troops who made the first landings, 6 June 1944. Four officers, (l to r) Lts B de la Tour, D Wells, J Vischer and Capt R Midwood, synchronise watches.**

before the landings started. If they didn't succeed they would be shelled themselves, by the warship HMS Arethusa.

The huge guns at Merville were just miles from the beaches of Sword, Juno and Gold, where the seaborne assault was to take place and posed the greatest threat to the invasion. Buried under 12ft-thick concrete, the four 75mm guns had the capability to engage Royal Navy warships out at sea and sink landing craft heading for the beaches.

RAF bombers had tried several times to destroy the concrete bunkers at Merville, but their precision bombing made no impression; now the task had been given to the Paras.

The 6th Airborne division was 8,500 strong and included the 3rd and 5th Parachute Brigades, as well as the 6th Air Landing Brigade of glider borne troops, who had been training at Netheravon. Their role was to seize or destroy several bridges over two rivers and the Caen canal, silence enemy positions in the area and secure the eastern flank of the beaches. Here the British Second Army was to come ashore, just a few hours later.

The 3rd Parachute Brigade had to land in the very heart of the enemy's defences and destroy the Troarn, Varaville, Robehomme and Bures bridges across the Dives river, while its 9th battalion hit Merville. At the same time, their colleagues in the 5th Parachute Brigade were given a similar task and briefed to hold the bridges north of the village of Ranville spanning the River Orne and the Caen canal, as well as preparing a landing zone for the glider troops.

More than 200 gliders were towed up into the skies of Britain during the night of June 5, along with a huge force of Dakota aircraft heading for what should have been, the most planned military action of the war.

Flak started to hit the aircraft and as pilots took avoiding action weaving across the sky, some Paras already hooked up and waiting to jump, were tossed out of the doors.

The entire force of 9 Para had been dropped off their DZ and Lt Col Otway could only assemble 150 men to commence his attack. He ordered his men to paint a skull and crossbones on the chest of their smocks as an identifying mark to recognise each other in the heat of the battle, which along with their blackened faces and helmets, served to scare the Germans.

After more of the battalion had arrived, one of the unit's officers sounded his hunting horn to start the assault on one of the most vital features of D-Day.

Para casualties were very heavy, but the Germans surrendered. Then just half an hour before the Navy were to start shelling the Merville guns, Otway fired a yellow flare to signal his unit's success.

Glider troops had been ordered to capture Pegasus bridge, which they did despite

Far right: Airborne troops land in Normandy on D-Day.
Left: Parachute troops apply 'war paint' before emplaning, 5 June 1944. *Below:* Camouflaged with blackened faces, paratroopers take up their positions in the aircraft.
Bottom: Unloading 'Charlie's Aunt' at Ranville, in a field which was under smallarms fire at the time. Note the poles in the background, erected for the purpose of stopping gliders.

Below: Glider troops beside the glider in which they were landed. Airborne forces in gliders did fine work by holding important bridges and engaging the enemy well inland. Bad weather delayed the invasion by 24 hours, but late on the night of 5 June, 250 gliders were towed into the skies over Britain. The pathfinders of 22nd Independent Parachute Company were tasked to mark the drop zone and guide the parachute and glider units, using special Eureka beacons.
Left: D-Day Normandy landing. Paratroopers had bicycles ready for the drop on Normandy.
Right: D-Day, Normandy. Paratroopers advancing to contact the enemy.

heavy enemy fire and constant counter attacks, which lasted days.

Arthur Brock, a Royal Engineer serving with Airborne Forces, was in one of three gliders which landed directly in the area of the bridge and owes his life to his Army pay book.

He was sent in to deal with mines, but instead, found himself in the thick of the fighting. He was showered by shrapnel from a shell blast, sending splinters of metal flying into his chest, but luckily, not him. His Army pay book took the blast and saved his life. 'I was very lucky, but others weren't so fortunate. The shelling went on for hours, I will never forget it, or my pals.'

Just four days after D-Day, the Germans attempted to push through the divisional area at Breville. A battle raged for hours and the enemy lost 200 dead and 150 prisoners to 13 Para, but still maintained their position, threatening to break through to the invasion beaches.

In the days that followed, 153 Infantry Brigade launched an assault on Breville, but were beaten off, suffering heavy casualties.

On June 12, the Germans launched two major attacks with armour support on 9 Para. The Battalion held its ground and beat off the assault, but by the end of the day, the unit was reduced to just 200 men.

Finally 12 Para with a company of 12 Devons and 22 Independent Parachute Company, were ordered to capture the village of Breville, in order to secure the division's sector, in defence of the beach head.

At a cost of 141 men, Breville was back in Allied possession and proved to be one of the most important battles of the invasion. Had it been lost the beaches could have been attacked and the war lost.

Chapter five

THE BATTLE FOR ARNHEM

Inset and *below:* Prior to departure. Members of 1st Para Brigade prepare for the airlift to Arnhem.

THE BATTLE FOR Arnhem had been planned as the spearhead of a powerful allied thrust through Holland and across the Rhine, using a massive airborne force to jump ahead of the ground troops to secure the route.

This 'airborne carpet' was to drop along the Eindhoven–Arnhem Road and seize bridges over the Rhine, which would provide the stepping stones for the Second Army's advance across the last barrier to Germany.

Within 48 hours of the drop, armoured columns of 30 Corps and other units, would dash 60 miles across the flat Dutch terrain and link up with the airborne units, before the enemy had chance to reinforce their defences.

Codenamed Operation Market Garden, the airborne assault took place on September 17, 1944, when 10,000 allied paratroopers filled the skies above Holland, unaware of the troubled times ahead of them and the fact that fewer than 3,000 would return.

Allied intelligence reports indicated that German morale was low and enemy forces in the area were weak, nothing could have been further from the truth. German spirits were, in fact, high, and an SS Panzer unit was in Arnhem, overhauling its tanks.

Despite losing aircraft, the drop had gone according to plan and the British airborne units were quickly away to their allotted tasks with the 1st Air Landing Reconnaissance Squadron, heading towards the bridges. But of the 320 gliders involved in the operation, 38 failed to arrive. Included in those casualties were the jeeps of the reconnaissance squadron.

The Germans had initially been taken by surprise and after landing at Renkum Common, eight miles west of Arnhem, the 1st Parachute Brigade set off in the direction of Arnhem, their objective – to seize the road and rail bridges across the Rhine.

Led by Lt Col Frost, 2 Para took the lower Oosterbeek road heading for Arnhem bridge, while 1 and 3 Para took separate routes in the same direction, only to be ambushed by German armoured units.

Now Lt Col Frost, the man who had led the attack on Bruneval and had seen action all over north Africa and Sicily, was at the forefront of action again. His 700 Paras marched to Arnhem and captured the northern end of the vital road bridge, only to meet a fierce attack from SS Panzer grenadiers as they tried to assault the southern side of the structure.

Earlier, before flying out to lead the Paras in their finest hour, Frost had ordered his golf clubs to be packed so he could enjoy himself after beating the Germans, but they had other ideas. To repulse the Paras' advance, they poured more SS troops into Arnhem, including three crack Panzer units, supported by heavy armour and well trained troops.

Frost, like the other battalion com-

manders, had been told that they only had to defend the bridge for 48 hours until 30 Corps arrived. But they couldn't get through and the Paras faced a bitter fight against Panzer tanks on their own.

At dawn on September 18, the Paras were rushed by a force of five armoured and seven tracked troop carriers, in an attempted assault by the Germans to take the bridge. All the vehicles were knocked out with anti-tank weapons. They burned all day under the eyes of the Paras and their enemy, blocking the bridge until the end of the battle.

After a full day of intense shelling,

attacks and counter attacks at the bridge, the Paras fixed bayonets and charged the Germans, who were preparing for another assault. They charged to the battle cry, of 'Whoa Mohammed', which had been adopted during the 2nd Battalion's service in north Africa, when an Arab used the term to slow his donkey.

Lt John Grayburn led his men across the bridge, to mount numerous counter attacks, despite being heavily outgunned by Panzer tanks and the ever increasing number of SS Panzer grenadiers.

Grayburn was injured twice, but refused to be evacuated and remained in the fore-

Left top: **Part of the 'airborne carpet'. 'Ten thousand allied paras filled the skies . . . fewer than 3,000 would return'.**
Left centre: **A paratrooper makes a bad landing at Arnhem.**
Above: **Amidst the action. Alan Wood, Correspondent of the *News Chronicle* and *Daily Express* types his report in a hollow at Oosterbeek.**

front of the fighting at Arnhem bridge until he was killed in action on the night of September 20, 1944. He was posthumously awarded the Victoria Cross for his actions. His citation read 'There is no doubt that, had it not been for this officer's inspiring leadership and personal bravery, the Arnhem bridge would not have been held for the time it was'.

The Germans rained firepower down on the northern side of the bridge, destroying every house and were amazed by the Paras refusal to surrender – instead the Red Berets responded by attacking at every opportunity.

On the third day, a short truce allowed the wounded to be taken into German captivity. Then the fighting resumed, until one by one the Paras ran out of ammunition and their position was overrun; just 100 men remained.

Today, General Frost CBE, DSO, MC and Bar, holds no bitterness towards his old commanders who were unprepared. He confines his criticism to the fact that 'our generals had an off day'.

'It slowly dawned on us that no help was coming. By the time we surrendered, we had 250 wounded, including myself. I'd been hit in the feet by shrapnel . . . In war, there are two things people always forget – how to care for the wounded and how to supply ammunition. We'd got only the bullets we carried on us'.

In action, Frost was a tough leader whose clear head in battle won the respect of every Paratrooper in the battalion. 'He didn't mix his words and seemed to inject confidence in everyone, even if you didn't like what he said. We would have followed him anywhere' said one Para.

The remains of the initial airborne force

had been forced to consolidate at Oosterbeek and they, with Frost and his men at Arnhem bridge, were taken prisoner – but only after having fired every round in their possession.

Despatch rider, Dennis Clay, had volunteered for 'special service' and having completed parachute training at Ringway, found himself serving in RASC Airborne Light Company. As a driver, he was detailed to fly into Arnhem by glider, ready to get access to his jeep. But cast off 10 miles short of Arnhem, the glider crash landed, the wings were ripped off and the aircraft turned over, everyone was killed – except Driver Clay.

The stunned Para was helped by a Dutchman, who told him there were five Germans in his home, who wanted to surrender. Clay took them prisoner and marched through the woods until he met

up with men from the Staffordshires of the 1st Air Landing Brigade.

'I'll never forget it, there I was on my own having just survived this crash and a bunch of Germans give themselves up to me.' Dennis Clay was later decorated.

There were many heroic actions recorded during Operation Market Garden and the bravery of the fifteen Army Chaplins who served with the 6th Airborne division, saved many lives. But only a handful of the chaplins survived. After the battle they stayed behind to tend the wounded and were captured almost straight away.

In total 7,167 men were listed as killed, missing or wounded at Arnhem, in an operation described by some as, 'a total disaster'. But after the battle, in which the Paras won five Victoria Crosses, the American General Dwight Eisenhower was full of praise for the airborne warriors.

He said, 'There has been no single performance by any unit that has more greatly inspired me or more excited my admiration than the nine day action by the 1st British Parachute Division between September 17 and 25'.

In December 1944, the German armies launched a massive counter attack through the forests of the Ardennes. The plan was aimed at splitting the Allied forces and pushing through a German advance fast and furious. Montgomery called for reinforcements and the 6th Airborne division, recently rested after their success in Normandy, were ordered to move at once and form a defensive line at crossing points on the River Meuse.

The enemy advance was quickly halted, but the Germans re-grouped at Bure and on January 13, 1945, the men of 13 Para were ordered to attack the village.

Above: Airborne soldiers captured during the Battle for Arnhem, 1944. Over 7,000 men were listed as killed, missing or wounded at Arnhem. Despite the losses, the action of the 1st Parachute Division earned high praise from General Eisenhower and their German enemies.
Left: British prisoners carrying a comrade on an improvised stretcher at Arnhem, September 21, 1944.

Chapter six

CROSSING THE RHINE

This picture was taken in a Dakota aircraft over Germany on March 24, 1945. It was the first aircraft to cross the Rhine.

Below: The scene as troops of the 6th Airborne Division land northwest of Wesel.
Far right upper: A paratrooper hangs in a tree near Wesel.
Far right lower: The signboard of Hamminkeln. The town was taken by troops of the 6th Airborne Division.

THE biggest and most successful airborne operation in history marked the beginning of the end for Germany, as Allied airborne troops mounted the final barrier and crossed the Rhine, in Operation Varsity.

In total, six parachute battalions, including the Canadians, of the 6th Airborne division, supported by glider troops from the Air Landing Brigade, dropped on March 24, 1945, as a complete force, avoiding the mistakes of Arnhem.

Together with the US 17th Airborne Division, the aim of the operation was to secure and deepen the bridgehead east of the Rhine and then advance across country to the Baltic coast, a journey of 350 miles. Their initial objectives were the high ground overlooking the crossing point at Diersfordter Wald and the road and rail bridges over the River Issel at Hamminkeln.

Flying in tight formation, 540 American

Dakota aircraft carried the 12 parachute battalions, five British, one Canadian and six from the US, closely followed by 1,300 gliders, packed with troops.

The Germans expected the invasion, and fighting on the DZs was heavy. By the end of the first day's action 1,078 men of the 6th Airborne Division had been either killed or wounded, with 50 aircraft and 11 gliders shot down.

Weather for the drop was perfect and almost everyone landed on their respective DZ, although some ended up in the trees

and were cut down by German machine guns as they fought to free themselves.

The 5th Parachute Brigade suffered heavily from casualties as mortar fire exploded in the skies around them during the drop. On the ground the enemy had occupied almost all of the nearby houses, but by late afternoon, the Brigades' three battalions had cleared them.

Within 24 hours, all objectives for the brigade had been achieved and as planned, the division was joined by ground forces of the 21st Army Group, for the advance across Germany. The bridges over the river were secured and the village of Hammin

keln captured, all objectives had been achieved within 24 hours.

Field Marshal Montgomery, who was by now the Colonel Commandant of the Parachute Regiment, wanted 6th Airborne to head the advance and this they did . . . on foot.

In support of the airborne troops were the tanks of the Grenadier Guards and three regiments of artillery. In just seven days they marched and fought their way to the Baltic port of Wismar and joined up with the leading elements of Russian troops.

On May 5, 1945, General Urquhart was warned to prepare to move his airborne men to Norway, where they were to ensure that the Germans observed the terms of the surrender. For the Paras it was yet another dangerous job. There were 35,000 Germans and just 6,000 airborne troops to monitor them.

Later the 1st Airborne Division was withdrawn to the UK and disbanded on August 26, 1945 – almost four years to the day after its formation.

Above: The 6th Airborne Division and Soviet troops meet near Wismar. The Russian girl soldier is the Russian Division telegraphist.
Far left: A British paratrooper, wearing his helmet and taking the opportunity to have a quick smoke, questions his German prisoner, captured during the Rhine Crossing.
Left: Men of the 6th Airborne Division advance on foot and bike through Brelingen, during the advance of the biggest and most successful airborne operation in history – Operation Varsity.

An NCO of 3 Para, of the 6th Airborne Division, observes above a road block near Haifa. The Division was deployed to the streets on internal security, as Arab-Jewish violence erupted.

Chapter seven

PALESTINE 1945 AND AFTER

58

ONLY months after the war in Europe had ended, the Paras found themselves in action again, this time manning a peaceline against Jewish terrorists whom, ironically, they had helped liberate.

The 6th Airborne Division went to Palestine in 1945 as an integral part of the Imperial Strategic Reserve for the Middle East, but soon found themselves deployed to the streets on internal security, as violence flared between Arab and Jewish communities.

With the holocaust over, thousands of Jews sought refuge in Palestine, but a British White Paper, drawn up in 1939, had limited Jewish immigration to 75,000, a figure which was soon exhausted.

To the Jews, the decision by the British to impose a restriction on the number of people entering their 'homeland', was inhuman and could only led to conflict, with extremist groups committed to armed attacks against the security forces.

For the Paras it was an unbelievable situation; only months earlier their actions had helped to liberate the Jewish prisoners of war, now they were being spat at and insulted by this same race.

In November 1945, Jews in Tel Aviv organised a huge and ugly riot in a bid to discredit the Paras and make them appear oppressors, after the 'Red Berets' were forced to return fire, causing casualties.

There were several terrorist groups, the Stern gang later became prominent as the

most violent and along with others, began to ambush police patrols using 'hit and run' tactics of guerrilla warfare. Bitterness deepened when the Stern gang shot dead seven paratroopers of 5th Parachute Battalion, gunning them down in cold blood.

The Jews hated the Red Berets and labelled them anti-semitic, as well as calling them *Kalionets*, their word for poppy . . . a red flower with a black heart.

No Para enjoyed Palestine. As one officer recalled, 'It was very unrewarding and unreal for soldiers, most of whom had taken part in heavy fighting across Europe, to find themselves being attacked by these people.

'It should not be forgotten that the actions of airborne troops helped to secure the liberation of many Jews, yet they suddenly

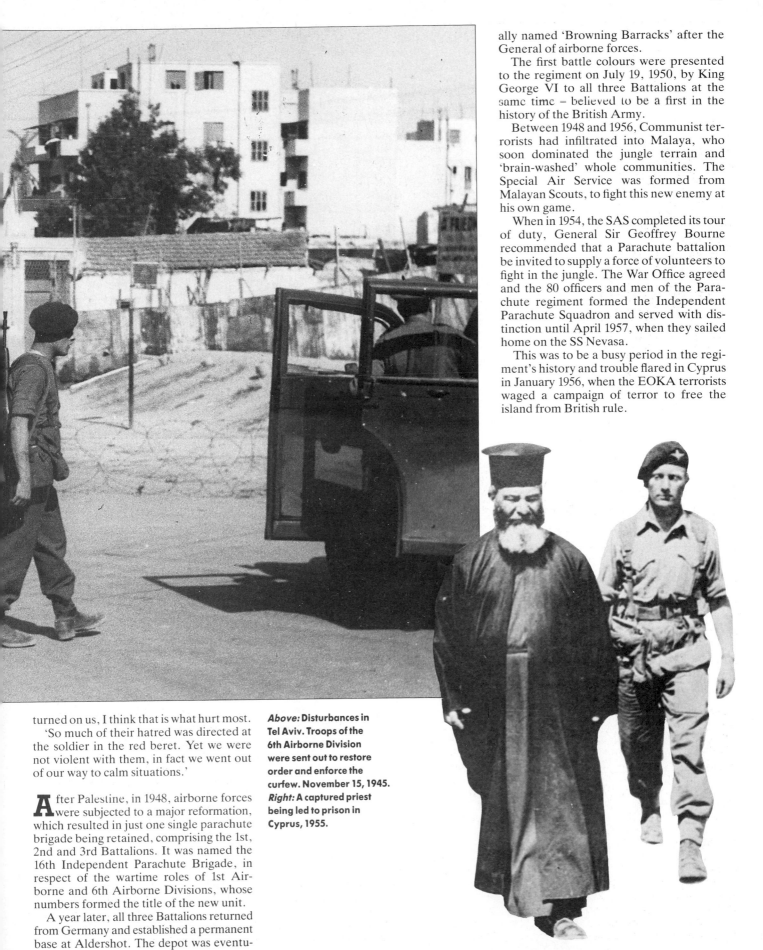

ally named 'Browning Barracks' after the General of airborne forces.

The first battle colours were presented to the regiment on July 19, 1950, by King George VI to all three Battalions at the same time – believed to be a first in the history of the British Army.

Between 1948 and 1956, Communist terrorists had infiltrated into Malaya, who soon dominated the jungle terrain and 'brain-washed' whole communities. The Special Air Service was formed from Malayan Scouts, to fight this new enemy at his own game.

When in 1954, the SAS completed its tour of duty, General Sir Geoffrey Bourne recommended that a Parachute battalion be invited to supply a force of volunteers to fight in the jungle. The War Office agreed and the 80 officers and men of the Parachute regiment formed the Independent Parachute Squadron and served with distinction until April 1957, when they sailed home on the SS Nevasa.

This was to be a busy period in the regiment's history and trouble flared in Cyprus in January 1956, when the EOKA terrorists waged a campaign of terror to free the island from British rule.

turned on us, I think that is what hurt most.

'So much of their hatred was directed at the soldier in the red beret. Yet we were not violent with them, in fact we went out of our way to calm situations.'

After Palestine, in 1948, airborne forces were subjected to a major reformation, which resulted in just one single parachute brigade being retained, comprising the 1st, 2nd and 3rd Battalions. It was named the 16th Independent Parachute Brigade, in respect of the wartime roles of 1st Airborne and 6th Airborne Divisions, whose numbers formed the title of the new unit.

A year later, all three Battalions returned from Germany and established a permanent base at Aldershot. The depot was eventu-

Above: Disturbances in Tel Aviv. Troops of the 6th Airborne Division were sent out to restore order and enforce the curfew. November 15, 1945. *Right:* A captured priest being led to prison in Cyprus, 1955.

60

The Air Adjt, Captain
Geoffrey Howlett (seated
in the jeep), organizes
the uncrating of supplies,
El Gamil, November 5,
1956.

THE most recent, and to date, the last combat drop by the Paras, took place at Suez, when they joined French forces to protect the shipping canal after Egypt's President Nasser 'nationalised' the international waterway.

In November 1956, Lt Col Paul Crook, commanding officer of the 3rd Battalion Parachute Regiment, was told to prepare his Cyprus based unit for an operation. But with the 'run-down' of airborne forces after

the war, equipment was in short supply.

The plan, jointly agreed with French military commanders, called for 3 Para to parachute into a 'hot DZ' – held by the enemy – where they expected to face a fierce battle against 2,000 Egyptian troops, who were supported by armour.

Operation Musketeer would need the element of total surprise if it was to succeed, and all 660 men had to be on the ground at El Gamil airfield and ready for action

within four and a half minutes.

Aircraft were covered in a coat of 'Gentian violet', a blue coloured medication, in a bid to camouflage them against the bright rays of the rising sun. In addition the airstrip at El Gamil was very narrow and the drop height had to be restricted to 700ft or less, in order to avoid soldiers being swept off the DZ by crosswinds.

A further move which was not popular with the Battalion, was the decision not to

wear reserve parachutes – due to the fact that they would not have the chance to use them at such low level.

The Brigade had hardly enough aircraft for a single battalion lift. The Hastings and Valettas were unable to carry heavy equipment and at that time, the new Beverley transporters were not yet available.

At 04.15 hours on November 5, 1956, 3 Para jumped in and although opposition was heavy, casualties were few. The unit medical officer, Lt Sandy Cavanagh, was shot in the eye as he descended to the DZ, as well as a dozen other injuries sustained on the ground.

The Egyptians had been supplied with Soviet weapons and on the second day a Russian Mig fighter strafed the Paras, causing two casualties. It was a 'one-off' incident, regarded as a show of strength by the Red Air Force against world opinion.

A sergeant, who was one of the first out

Above: **Col P E Crook, 3 Para, and his Tac HQ move into the airport buildings at El Gamil Airfield, Port Said, after an airborne assault, November 5, 1956.**

of the door at Suez, still remembers his concern for the unexpected. 'We were nervous, nobody really knew what to expect, but as soon as we left the aircraft, they started firing at us . . . The airfield was covered with oil drums to stop aircraft landing and once we had cleared it, we made our way to Port Said. There was quite a bit of fighting and we took a few injuries, but nothing to shout about'.

At Port Said, 2 Para came ashore, but within a week a ceasefire had been announced and the regiment pulled out, heading back to Cyprus. World opinion had forced Britain and France to withdraw their forces.

The Battalion had acted in the highest traditions of the Parachute regiment, but the regiment had not been prepared for the operation and new equipment was desperately needed.

Worse was to come. When they arrived back in Cyprus the Military Police were ready to search the Paras after it had been alleged that the French airborne troops sold weapons to EOKA terrorists.

The Suez operation had been mounted after a series of incidents which began when President Gamel Abdel Nasser demanded the withdrawal of all British military units from Egypt.

Within weeks of them leaving in March 1956, the President took full control of the Suez shipping canal. Britain and France held major shares in the Suez canal company, a business which raised $35 million in profits a year. But Nasser impounded the company, using its funds to finance his country's Aswan High Dam project.

Both the French and the British Governments were incensed and after protesting, eventually took the issue to the United Nations Security Council.

Nasser refused Israel the use of the canal, a contravention of the 1888 Treaty, which guaranteed free passage to all States and in reaction, the tiny Jewish state promised military action against him.

On October 29, Israel launched Operation Kadesh and two days later, the RAF began four days of bombing attacks, which destroyed the Egyptian Air Force. On November 5, the Anglo-French airborne force flew in to seize key locations in Port Said.

Continued unrest in Cyprus called for increased internal security duties against EOKA in February 1957, with the

Above: **Making way for the jeep in rough and hilly country, men of the Parachute Brigade push forward during an exercise with the Arab Legion in Jordan. The soldiers, their jeeps and equipment have been parachuted in from the Canal Zone in Egypt.** *Far left:* **3 Para move into El Gamil Airfield.** *Left:* **Operation Musketeer Drop Zone.**

2nd Battalion remaining on the island, while 1 and 3 Para returned to Aldershot.

In 1958, 16 Para Brigade was flown at short notice to Cyprus as civil war broke out in Lebanon. In the event, American forces went in, but within days King Hussein of Jordan asked Britain for assistance following a coup in Iraq which threatened Jordan. The Brigade was flown into Amman to secure the airport and support the King; they remained there for three months. Their presence alone had averted further trouble.

In June 1961, the Paras joined their cousins in the Royal Marines, as a deterrent force, deployed on the border of Kuwait, after Iraq threatened to invade the oil rich country.

Again, their presence was enough to avoid conflict and for the next six years, until 1967, parachute battalions were to be based in the Persian Gulf as a 'fire brigade' force, to react to any conflict in the region.

It was also the first time the Paras had been able to take their wives and families with them, based in sunny Bahrain.

An escalation of trouble yet again in Cyprus in 1964, now an independent state, saw 1 Para move in to support a United Nations peace keeping force, replacing their red berets for the first time since 1942, with the light blue of the UN.

The battalion was awarded the UN medal and today British troops are still supporting the United Nations force in Cyprus. All three battalions take their turn to serve with the UN force in a rota controlled by the Ministry of Defence, which falls as an addition to regular deployments to Ulster and the Falklands.

A Paratrooper faces the
hatred of the IRA while on
patrol in Northern
Ireland, in the Army's
longest operational
campaign.

Chapter ten

THE LONGEST CAMPAIGN

WHEN the first battalion arrived in Ulster they were unaware that they were the forerunners of the Army's longest operational campaign which would see the regiment facing some of the most sickening violence in history.

They were sent in by the then Labour Prime Minister, Harold Wilson, at the request of the Northern Ireland Government, following months of sectarian violence between rival Catholic and Protestant communities of Londonderry.

Just weeks after the first troops arrived on August 14, 1969, the 1st Battalion was deployed to the Province for an emergency tour of duty, codenamed Operation Banner, serving in the Shankhill district of Belfast. Their job was to protect the Catholic community from extremist Protestant attacks and they were clapped and cheered whenever they entered Republican areas.

Within 12 months the atmosphere had changed. The Paras found the attacks being directed at them in the form of shooting, petrol bombs and riots.

Cakes and buns earlier handed out to the Red Berets by Catholic housewives as a thank you for protecting them were still passed out, but now contained powdered glass and rat poison.

The Paras were accused by the IRA of excessive 'use of force' in a propaganda campaign to discredit the regiment and the British Army. In fact it was the Parachute regiment who were the first unit to build a 'hearts and minds' relationship with the community. But the IRA increased its reign of terror over the community with a series of 'stage-managed' events against the Army, which convinced the Catholics that they should turn to the IRA for protection.

The regiment lost its first man in 1971 when Sgt Mick Willets was killed by an IRA bomb at the Springfield Road police station. A suitcase was thrown in the doorway as a family walked into the station. He stood in the doorway and used his body as a protective shield while the two adults and their children escaped, sacrificing his own life to save them – a fact which raised not even a gesture of thanks from the community.

Above: Troops of Support Company carry out a 'search sweep' during Operation Water Baby, April 1971.
Upper right: A quieter moment for members of 2 Para in Belfast.
Centre right: In the beginning, the Paras enjoyed a caring, protective role in the Catholic community.
Lower right: A 'Red Beret' shares a secret with a local resident.

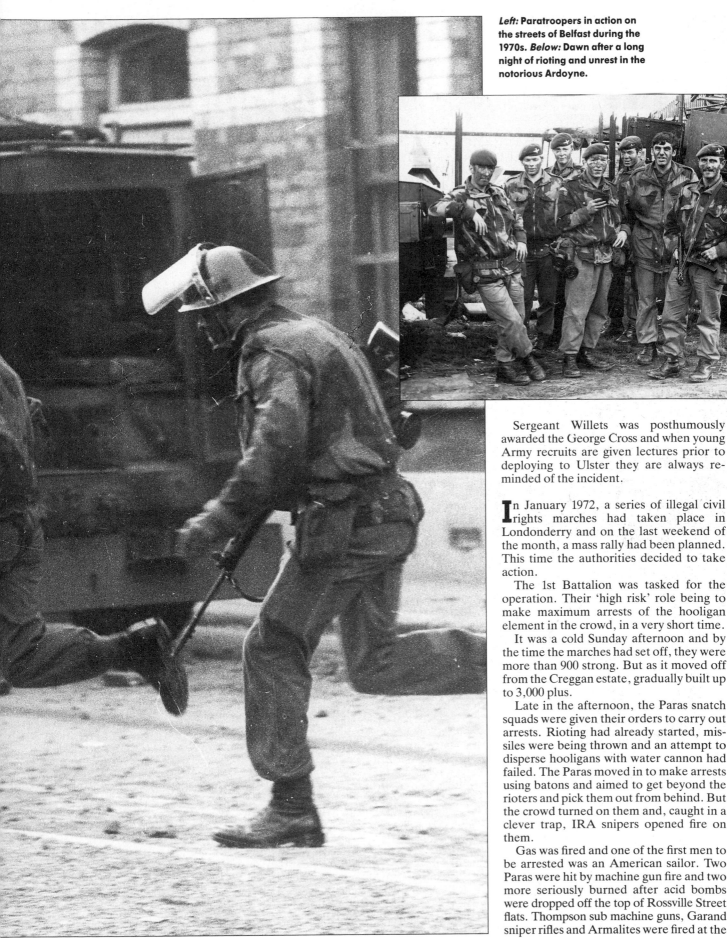

Left: Paratroopers in action on the streets of Belfast during the 1970s. *Below:* Dawn after a long night of rioting and unrest in the notorious Ardoyne.

Sergeant Willets was posthumously awarded the George Cross and when young Army recruits are given lectures prior to deploying to Ulster they are always reminded of the incident.

In January 1972, a series of illegal civil rights marches had taken place in Londonderry and on the last weekend of the month, a mass rally had been planned. This time the authorities decided to take action.

The 1st Battalion was tasked for the operation. Their 'high risk' role being to make maximum arrests of the hooligan element in the crowd, in a very short time.

It was a cold Sunday afternoon and by the time the marches had set off, they were more than 900 strong. But as it moved off from the Creggan estate, gradually built up to 3,000 plus.

Late in the afternoon, the Paras snatch squads were given their orders to carry out arrests. Rioting had already started, missiles were being thrown and an attempt to disperse hooligans with water cannon had failed. The Paras moved in to make arrests using batons and aimed to get beyond the rioters and pick them out from behind. But the crowd turned on them and, caught in a clever trap, IRA snipers opened fire on them.

Gas was fired and one of the first men to be arrested was an American sailor. Two Paras were hit by machine gun fire and two more seriously burned after acid bombs were dropped off the top of Rossville Street flats. Thompson sub machine guns, Garand sniper rifles and Armalites were fired at the

Paras in a series of separate fire fights, which lasted for over an hour.

The Paras engaged armed terrorists in what was a straightforward ambush by the IRA, who attempted to use the cover of the crowd as protection. When the shooting had stopped, 13 gunmen were dead and another 16 injured.

One Para said the entire operation had been mounted by the IRA who, expecting casualties, had prepared a makeshift first aid post inside the flats. 'They expected to kill half a dozen soldiers and fill the front pages of newspapers'.

It is widely believed that as many as 20 gunmen died during the fire fight, but were taken away to be buried elsewhere for fear that forensic science would have proved that they had been firing weapons. The Widgery Report exonerated the Paras from IRA claims that they had fired indiscriminately at a crowd and of opening fire before they themselves were fired upon.

For the Battalion they had simple done their job. Having been ambushed, they returned fire and the world's press dubbed the event 'Bloody Sunday'. It was a day the IRA would never forget.

Just a month later the IRA bombed the officers' mess of 16th Para Brigade in Aldershot, killing seven people. Among the victims were five women, a gardener and a Catholic padre.

Throughout 1970, the regiment became the top target of the IRA, after the Paras scored a series of successes against the terrorists, in a period when they clocked up more tours than any other unit.

Driving through Whiterock one evening, a 3 Para section suddenly became the target of an elaborate IRA attempt to kill a patrol, by baiting them to leave their vehicles and 'follow up' an incident.

The driver, who for security reasons cannot be named, saw what he thought was a discarded cigarette end flash over his windscreen, but instantly realised it was a blast bomb. Both Land Rovers pulled over and as the device exploded the crews jumped out to chase two men seen standing in a nearby alley. As they approached them a taxi pulled up and a gunman with a Thompson sub-machine gun opened fire on them. He was killed in the exchange of fire.

Since then there have been hundreds of incidents in which the IRA have used enticing tactics to draw the Paras and other units into a 'come-on' situation where they can ambush them.

The worst incident for the regiment, in Northern Ireland, took place in the late 1970s when a patrol was attacked at Warrenpoint Castle in South Armagh.

A road alongside a border river was regularly monitored by the Paras and other regiments, including the RUC, to prevent terrorists from planting bombs.

But at some point the Provisionals planted a huge bomb alongside the road, possibly in milk churns, on the day of their attack. On August 27, 1979, the IRA ambushed a combined Para and Queen's Own Highlanders vehicle convoy as they passed the castle.

In total 18 men were killed, 16 of them Paras, in a tragic attack. On the same day the IRA murdered Lord Mountbatten who was on a fishing holiday in Northern Ireland.

Since 1969, the regiment has lost 29 men in Ulster and received more than 16 gallantry awards, including Sgt Willet's George Cross.

In more than 20 years of trouble in Ulster, the politicians have presented their solutions and theories to the problems, but little has changed and today Paratroopers are still serving in Ulster.

To date the sum total of the regiment's service in the Province amounts to 10 years of service.

Above: 'Bloody Sunday', January 1972. As many as 13 gunmen died and another 16 were injured. It was a day the IRA would never forget.
Left: Paras, still wearing their Red Berets, make an arrest during the Londonderry riot.
Right: An ever-watchful eye . . . from soldier and civilian.

Men of 3 Para aboard a
landing craft on San
Carlos Waters.

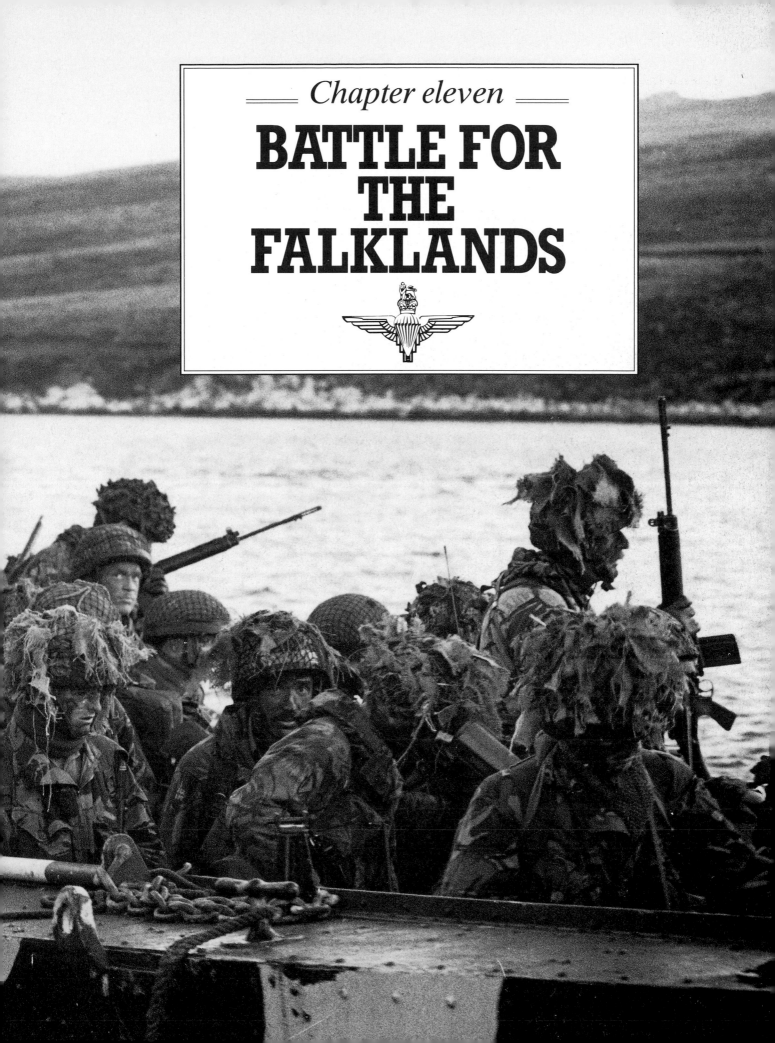

Chapter eleven

BATTLE FOR THE FALKLANDS

'READY FOR ANYTHING' has never had more meaning to the Paras 'than in 1982 when Argentina invaded the Falklands. Within days the standby Battalion had been recalled from leave and were heading for the South Atlantic.

First away was 3 Para, joining their green beret cousins of the Royal Marines aboard the SS Canberra, for a 3,000-mile journey to assault the Falklands beaches which was to be followed by a battle march across the island to regain control.

Embarking on the ferry MV Norland, 2 Para quickly followed and on May 21, the force made amphibious landings at San Carlos and Ajax Bay. For the next week air attacks against the beachhead took place daily.

On May 26, 2 Para under the command of Lt. Col. 'H' Jones, otherwise known as Col. 'H', was ordered by the brigade commander Brigadier Julian Thompson, to move south and engage the Argentinian strategic reserve and the airfield on the Darwin–Goose Green border.

The attack began in the early hours of May 28, with Naval and artillery support. But by daylight it was clear the enemy's defences were much stronger than reported.

In order to get a true picture of what was happening, 'H' Jones went forward himself to ensure that the thrust of his Bat-

Above: Soldiers of 3 Para and Royal Marines set sail from Southampton aboard the SS Canberra for the South Atlantic in 1982. *Left:* A young Para. *Right:* Men of 3 Para take part in helicopter drills aboard SS Canberra en route to the South Atlantic.

talion's assault was not lost at this most vital point. Supported by his reconnaissance party, he went further forward and spotted the source of the enemy firepower, which was well dug in and threatening to cause more casualties to 2 Para.

Colonel 'H' seized a machine gun, then charged the enemy position and although hit, continued his charge before being hit again, falling a few feet from the trench he had assaulted. A helicopter piloted by a young Royal Marine officer attempted to fly in to evacuate the wounded colonel, but was shot down in the battle, killing its crew.

His courage and leadership won Colonel 'H' the Victoria Cross, in what was the Paras first open confrontation since 1945.

Colonel H's widow, Sara, today lives with the pride and pain of losing her husband, but feels 2 Para's victory was the most important battle of the war. 'If H hadn't pulled that battle together, I believe the whole Falklands campaign might have been a different story. I am enormously proud of what he did. In fact, proud isn't a strong enough word'.

Shortly after 'H' Jones was killed, a company swept through and attacked the enemy, who quickly surrendered. Their spirits devastated by the courageous display of the 'Red Devils' leader.

Major Chris Keeble took command of the battalion and fought on to surround Goose Green, with the surrender of the Argentines on May 29. The Paras had expected a couple of hundred prisoners. Instead 1,350 Argentines gave themselves up, more than 250 were dead and 140 wounded. The Paras had been fighting at odds three to one against. The battalion had suffered 15 dead and 40 injured.

One of the unsung heroes of Goose Green was Major Colin Connor, who, isolated behind enemy lines, relayed vital information back to his Colonel's battle plan prior to attacking the airfield.

By the time the Battalion had moved off Sussex mountain for Goose Green, he was already stalking the enemy. In freezing conditions and without food or water, Colin crawled five miles to note enemy positions.

For 14 hours he lay still as Argentine lookouts scanned the hills for signs of an advance. Finally, disregarding his own safety, he called in an air strike on enemy positions.

He survived to become one of the youngest soldiers in the British Army to receive the Military Cross. 'I was only doing what I had been trained for. Any man in 2 Para would have done the same' said Major Connor.

The 3rd Battalion mounted a night attack on Mount Longdon on June 11 and encountered heavy resistance. With bayonets fixed, B Company's No. 4 platoon found themselves advancing under heavy fire.

Sergeant Ian McKay and the platoon

Top: Men of 3 Para go ashore in Navy landing craft at San Carlos Water. *Above and far right:* The Argentines surrendered on May 29 — the Paras had expected a couple of hundred prisoners — 1,350 Argentines gave themselves up. The Paras had been fighting at odds of three to one against. *Right:* Men of 3 Para Regimental Aid Post tend the wounded of both sides at the base of Mount Longdon.

commander moved forward to see where the fire was coming from. The commander was shot and Sgt McKay took over and immediately decided the reconnaissance patrol should change role and attack in order to eliminate the enemy.

Taking three men with him, he broke cover and charged the machine gun post, meeting a hail of gunfire. The Corporal was seriously wounded, a private killed and another wounded, but McKay continued the attack on his own throwing grenades into the Argentine position.

Sergeant McKay died at the point of victory by enemy fire, falling into the bunker he had captured single-handed. His outstanding courage won him the Victoria Cross – the second for the regiment in the Falklands.

Following the capture of Mount Longdon, 3 Para's mortars and fire teams supported 2 Para's attack on Wireless Ridge. Later 2 Para became the first troops to march into Port Stanley.

The regiment was awarded 2 Victoria Crosses (Posthumous) and 68 other decorations as well as four battle honours.

Left: Soldiers of the 2 Para make their way through Stanley, after fighting their way across the island. *Inset:* Young Argentines are taken prisoner. *Below left:* A quick wash and brush up for troops of the 3 Para. *Below:* Troops and citizens of Port Stanley raise the union and battalion flags.

A soldier of 5 Airborne Brigade packs away his parachute, after jumping onto Salisbury Plain.

TODAY Britain's airborne forces have an exclusive role operating as an 'out of area' strike force, ready to be deployed anywhere outside the NATO area. Only twelve years ago the future of such a force looked very much in doubt, after the 16th Parachute Brigade was disbanded and less priority was given to the 'parachute' role.

Then in 1982, the only operational force available to mount an immediate deployment was the Royal Marines' 3 Commando Brigade – who commanded the assault to retake the Falklands.

As a direct result of lessons learned from the South Atlantic campaign, the Army's 5 Brigade, which had been shipped out to join Operation Corporate aboard the QEII, was renamed and given a more important profile.

On November 14, 1983, the unit was re-titled 5 Airborne Brigade and was set to include two parachute trained battalions, supported by 20 specialist units, forming a highly mobile reaction force.

The 5,600 strong Brigade operates on a system first adopted by the wartime commanders of the 1st and 6th Airborne divisions, with a combined force of parachute and air-landing soldiers.

The formation of the airborne group draws together a wealth of skills across the military spectrum, which enable it to remain self-sufficient until additional forces arrive. It has a dual role as the Army's 'out of area' force in peace and the only all regular group to remain in the UK for the defence of the mainland in the event of war.

The Brigade is on a permanent state of

Chapter twelve
5 AIRBORNE BRIGADE

alert ready to spearhead the safe evacuation of British nationals from a hostage situation and support friendly Governments against threatened military action. To the observer, these roles may appear to be unsuited, but the Brigade's ability to operate over long distances at short notice, gives it the perfect pedigree for such a job.

Since its formation, a number of exercises have taken place in the Middle East, operating on the scenario of a 'friendly' country being invaded by a hostile neighbour.

Its structure includes a small unit of

parachute trained soldiers from the Household Cavalry equipped with Scorpian, a light armoured recce vehicle, which provides firepower for the force and a sharp change of role from their more familiar ceremonial duties.

In addition, the Brigade has its own medics, engineers, artillery, logistics and pathfinder unit, as well as an infantry battalion attached to it, which is trained to fly into battle by helicopter.

The 35-strong pathfinder unit is drawn from parachute trained soldiers serving with

the Brigade – all are volunteers and must pass a rigorous selection course on Dartmoor before going to RAF Brize Norton for free-fall training.

At the Parachute Training Centre they are taught the art of HALO, High Altitude Low Opening, which involves leaving the aircraft at 20,000ft and free-falling below radar, before deploying their canopy.

Once on the ground, their job is to mark a drop zone for the remainder of the Battalion to follow, in exactly the same role as the wartime independent parachute units.

THE Special Air Service Regiment has remained a unit on its own since its inception in the western desert, although it works closely with Airborne Forces. Today almost half of its men are drawn from the Parachute regiment.

Based at Hereford, 'the regiment' as it is known within the British Army, has been the subject of mass media coverage since it was called on to storm the Iranian embassy in May 1980.

Today the balaclava image of the SAS has given the elite unit a reputation akin to being 'military surgeons', and whenever there is a crisis, the Press call for the regiment to fly in and 'cut-out' the cyst of trouble.

Much of the rumour and story telling about the SAS has developed because the public still know very little about these men, their activities or their methods, other than the fact that entry is only for the fittest in mind and body.

The regiment's selection process has been described as the 'most brutal' training in the world. But anyone who has attempted the four-week selection and raced to pass the tests in badge week, will confirm that instructors never hound candidates.

A veteran instructor says: 'We want people to do well and will help them. But we will never physically help them or shout words of encouragement, that would defeat the object of being here. The aim is for the

The siege of the Iranian Embassy was ended when the SAS went in. Five of the six terrorists were killed.

Chapter thirteen

SPECIAL AIR SERVICE

man to pass on his own ability.

'We are not here to push people into a role that they are not prepared for, that's not our style. We have a high percentage of Paras who come here and tend to do well, possibly because the two regiments are so closely related.

'But that isn't to say that every Para who comes here will pass. There are a lot who fail. But we believe it is better to have tried and failed than never to have tried at all.'

A hardcore of 'badged' soldiers form the three operational squadrons of 22 Special Air Service regiment and are supported by individual specialists units, often from parachute units. They include communications experts from the Royal Signals and medics from the Royal Army Medical Corps, all of whom must be parachute-trained before being considered for attachment.

The formation of the regiment dates back to the Long Range Desert Group in north Africa when 'L' Detachment was created in July 1941, to carry out covert operations behind enemy lines, a role still maintained by today's SAS.

The idea for this small commando style unit was proposed by Lt David Stirling, a young officer serving under Brigadier Laycock in north Africa. Despite initial opposition to his plan, Stirling secured the approval of General Auchinleck and quickly recruited his first crew of seven officers and sixty men.

The first SAS operation took place on November 17, 1941. It was an airborne assault behind the lines at a German airfield. But due to a sandstorm, the team was dropped off course and the mission was a complete failure.

Later in daring raids, deep into enemy lines, they destroyed more than 170 aircraft and in 1943, the 1st SAS regiment was formed with a strength of 1,100 men. Later the 2nd SAS was created, but neither was related to the Special Air Service Battalions formed in 1940.

In Europe the SAS carried out 43 operations between June 6 and October 31, 1944, with outstanding success. Throughout the war years they provided reliable intelligence including the location of some very important targets for the RAF.

After the war the 1st and 2nd SAS regiments were formed into the 21st SAS (volunteers), combining the numbers of the original units. In 1952 the Malayan scouts (an SAS unit), were renamed 22nd SAS and made available for regular service.

Demands on the regiments resulted in its expansion and by 1963 it consisted of three squadrons. They saw active service in Aden, Borneo and Oman, before being deployed to Ulster in 1976.

Their expertise in covert warfare has scored a hat trick of successes against the IRA and attracted worldwide demand from 'friendly' Governments for their troops to be 'SAS' trained.

The West German police unit GSG9, called on the SAS for assistance when an airliner full of German nationals was hijacked and taken to Mogadishu. Later the Dutch authorities asked the regiment for help when Moluccan terrorists held a train-load of passengers hostage.

The most famous episode in the regiment's history, flashed across television screens in 1980, was when in full anti-terrorist kit, they were sent in to rescue hostages at the Iranian embassy. All the terrorists were killed.

In the Falklands they led the attack to retake the islands, having landed in the south Atlantic weeks before the main Task Force arrived.

Then in March 1985, the SAS hit the IRA again, killing three terrorists in Gibraltar, who had been planning to blow up the band of the Royal Anglian regiment, during the 'Changing of the Keys' ceremony on the Rock.

Having already suffered a major setback when the SAS killed two of their active service units at Loch Goil, the Provisionals launched a backlash of mainland incidents and in September 1990, they attempted to kill the former Governor of Gibraltar, Sir Peter Terry, who had signed the documents that led to the SAS action.

In the most recent of international incidents, men from the regiment flew into Saudi and co-ordinated the covert surveillance of Iraqi troops on the Kuwait border. Armed with the latest in satellite communication equipment they quickly set up direct radio links with London.

A rifle, a Para's helmet and a jam jar of daffodils mark the spot where Sergeant Ian McKay, of 3 Para, fell on Mount Longdon.

Lance Sergeant John Baskeyfield.

Flight Lt David Samuel Lord.

Captain Lionel Ernest Queripel.

Major Robert Henry Cain.

Lt John Grayburn.

Corporal Frederick Topham.

Chapter fourteen

VC'S AWARDED TO AIRBORNE FORCES

THE Victoria Cross was created for valour and extreme courage beyond that normally expected of a British serviceman in the face of the enemy.

Since the medal was minted 136 years ago, only 1,354 have been awarded, eight of them being made to officers and men of the Parachute regiment and Airborne Forces.

Five of the Victoria Crosses awarded to Airborne Forces were made in recognition of outstanding valour and courage at Arnhem, in which more than 7,000 men were reported missing, wounded or killed.

On September 20, 1944, during the battle of Arnhem, Lance Sergeant John Baskeyfield of the Staffordshire regiment, was in charge of an anti-tank gun at Oosterbeek. He and his crew knocked out two Tiger tanks as the enemy made a heavy advance, killing all his gun team. But despite being severely wounded in the leg, he continued on his own, to fire the gun, as the enemy launched another attack. He succeeded in firing two rounds, before being killed in a hail of shell fire. His action earned him one of the first VCs for airborne forces.

Pilot David Samuel Lord was dropping supplies at Arnhem on September 19, 1944, when his aircraft was hit and set alight by enemy fire, just minutes from the drop zone. He continued with his mission to resupply ground forces and ignored his own safety, having ordered his crew to bale out – his Dakota crashed.

Captain Lionel Ernest Queripel commanded a company at Arnhem, when he came under heavy fire on September 19. Pinned down by fire and himself wounded in the face, he carried an injured NCO to the Aid Post. He then returned to his men and destroyed two enemy machine guns and captured an anti-tank gun. Later, although wounded in both arms, he inspired his men to beat off attacks from the Germans.

Armed with just a PIAT light anti-tank weapon, Major Robert Henry Cain immobilised a Tiger Tank, then in the following days he knocked out three more. When his company's position was attacked, Major Cain, by superb leadership and with just a two-inch mortar continued his assault in a bid to demoralise the enemy.

At Arnhem bridge, 2 Para found themselves under heavy fire from SS Panzer Grenadiers, and Lt John Grayburn led his men in two assaults over the bridge. Though twice wounded, he refused to be evacuated and insisted on leading the attacks. Had it not been for the action of this man, Arnhem bridge may not have been held for as long as it was. He was killed on the night of September 20.

During the Rhine Crossing in March 1945, Corporal Frederick Topham of the 1st Canadian Parachute Battalion, constantly exposed himself to enemy fire in his efforts to treat and evacuate the wounded.

More than 40 years passed before the Victoria Cross would be awarded to the Paras again in the Falklands campaign of 1982.

Sergeant Ian McKay of 3 Para, charged an enemy machine gun post which had been pinning down his comrades, and pressed home his attack, throwing grenades into the enemy position at Mount Longdon.

The commanding officer of 2 Para, Lt Colonel 'H' Jones, found his Battalion bogged down at Goose Green after hours of fighting. Assessing the need to break the stalemate and with total disregard for his own life, he charged the nearest enemy position.

Both men became the first to be awarded the Victoria Cross since World War Two.

Sergeant Ian McKay.

Lt Colonel 'H' Jones.

Right: A cameo of the action by men of 2 Para at Arnhem Bridge in September 1944 has been carefully constructed. *Below right:* A wartime jeep and motorbike crated to be dropped by parachute with the Paras. *Below:* Insignia and equipment retained in a unique collage of memorabilia.

The museum covers changes in Para uniform in the past 50 years and details weapons used by the Red Berets, such as the SLR, far right, and the GPMG, below.

The museum was originally established just six years after the formation of Airborne Forces in the Officers Mess at Corunna barracks in Aldershot. It was so successful that by 1952 it was too big and had to be moved. Later when the Parachute Regiment moved to Browning barracks a special area was set aside for it.

But like many military museums, it is suffering from a lack of space and in 1992 is due to move to a brand new Military Museum centre at Rushmoor arena.

Chapter fifteen

AIRBORNE MUSEUM

THE history of Airborne Forces has been preserved in a unique museum at the regiment's depot in Browning Barracks and was opened by one of the Paras greatest admirers, Field Marshal Montgomery.

The museum records the five decades of British Paras, from their inception in June 1940, to the present day with wartime clothing, insignia and exhibits displaying the Red Beret's battles.

Glider operations are heavily represented and the cockpits of a Hotspur and Horsa in their original state are on view, together with a vast array of airborne equipment developed during the pioneering years.

The key to Hitler's bunker, retrieved shortly after the Russian occupation of Berlin and the sword of office of the Luftwaffe commander Herman Goering are also on display.

From Tragino to the streets of Ulster, the museum's attention to detail has created a mountain of knowledge and is often consulted by film-makers and military experts seeking the 'true facts'.

The Parachute regiment has enlisted the support of a mascot since 1950, when 1 Para were presented with a black New Forest pony and ever since the Red Berets have always had a mascot.

From 'Bruneval' to 'Ringway', the names of these mascots have always been significant to regimental history and on April 15, 1955, all three mascots of the regular battalions were paraded in front of the Duke of Edinburgh.

Due to rising costs and accommodation problems, the initial plan to have a pony mascot for each unit was scrapped in 1965.

When the Paras marched through the streets of London on June 22, 1990, to celebrate their 50 years of glory, Pegasus the mascot led the parade of 3000 Red Berets in their proudest hour.

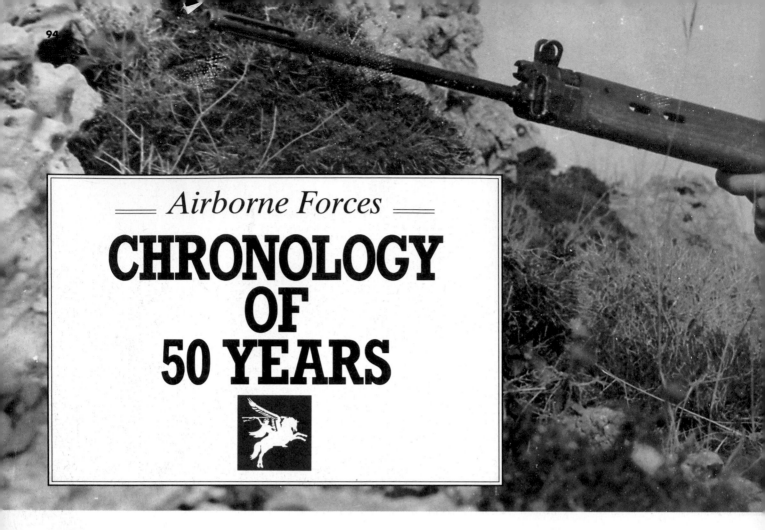

Airborne Forces
CHRONOLOGY OF 50 YEARS

22 June 1940 British Airborne Forces officially formed after Prime Minister Winston Churchill calls for a Corps of 5,000 parachute soldiers.

8 July 1940 Ground training commences at the Central Landing Establishment, RAF Ringway.

13 July 1940 First parachute descents recorded at Ringway.

10 Feb 1941 First airborne operation. Paras blow up the Tragino Aqueduct in Italy.

6 Aug 1941 'L' Detachment Special Air Service formed in the Middle East, under the command of Capt Stirling.

15 Sept 1941 Formation of 1st Parachute Brigade under Brigadier R Gale.

29 Oct 1941 Brigadier Frederick 'boy' Browning appointed commander of Airborne Forces as Major General.

1 Nov 1941 1st Airborne Division formed.

21 Dec 1941 Formation of the Army Air Corps and Glider Pilot regiment.

15 Jan 1942 Formation of No. 38 Wing RAF.

27 Feb 1942 Bruneval Raid. First battle honour.

1 Aug 1942 Formation of the Parachute regiment.

12 Nov 1942 3 Para capture Bone airfield, North Africa. First battalion strong operational drop.

19 Nov 1942 Operation Freshman — Paras executed by Germans after ill-fated raid.

19 Dec 1942 Paras earn the name 'Red Devils' from their German opponents in north Africa and spend months fighting in the desert.

27 March 1943 1st Parachute Brigade in action at Tamara, north Africa.

3 May 1943 6th Airborne division formed. Training starts at Netheravon.

9 July 1943 1st Air Landing Brigade capture Ponte Grande bridge, Sicily.

13 July 1943 1st Parachute brigade operation at Primosole bridge — battle honour.

6 June 1944 6th Airborne division secure left flank of Allied beach invasion.

12 July 1944 12 Para captures Breville and prevents the beach-head being attacked.

15 Aug 1944 Independent Parachute brigade see service in southern France, Operation Dragoon.

17 Sept 1944 Arnhem. 1st Airborne division, 2 Para cut off at the 'bridge'.

12 Oct 1944 4 Para seize Megara airfield for operation in Greece.

24 Dec 1944 6th Airborne division deployed to Ardennes.

3 Jan 1945 13 Para captures Bures in Ardennes.

24 March 1945 6th Airborne division — Rhine Crossing.

21 Sept 1945 6th Airborne fly into Palestine.

15 Nov 1945 1st Airborne division disbanded.

June 1948 2nd Para Brigade reforms in Germany as 16th Parachute Brigade.

Aug 1948 6th Airborne disbanded after Palestine.

19 July 1950 King George VI presents first colours to all three battalions.

Jan 1956 16th Para Brigade deployed to Cyprus. EOKA.

5 Nov 1956 3 Para parachute into El Gamil airfield. Suez.

1 Sept 1957 Glider Pilot Regiment renamed Army Air Corps.

June 1958 16th Parachute brigade fly into Jordan.

June 1961 2 Para deployed to Kuwait after Iraq threatens to invade.

May 1964 3 Para deployed to Radfan.

May 1964 2 Para on operations in Borneo.

Dec 1964 Cyprus – UN duties.

Oct 1965 3 Para – Guiana on IS duties.

29 Nov 1967 1 Para cover withdrawal from Aden.

6 June 1968 Browning barracks, Aldershot, new home of Para depot. Opened by Daphne du Maurier, wife of the late General Browning.

Nov 1969 2 Para – IS duties in Anguilla. Awarded Wilkinson Sword of Peace.

Nov 1969 1 Para deployed to Northern Ireland.

May 1971 All 3 battalions serving in Ulster.

25 May 1971 First Para killed in Ulster. Sgt Willetts of 3 Para.

30 Jan 1972 Bloody Sunday – 1 Para attacked by IRA gunmen. 13 terrorists shot dead. Five Paras injured.

22 Feb 1972 Officers' mess 16th Para brigade bombed by IRA. The victims included 5 women, a gardener and a Catholic padre.

31 July 1972 Operation Motorman – 1 and 2 Para involved in clearing of 'no-go' areas.

15 July 1974 All three regular battalions, including 4th (volunteer) receive second set of colours at Aldershot.

March 1975 Defence Review calls for reduced Para role.

31 March 1977 16th Parachute Brigade disbanded and replaced with 6th Field Force.

June 1977 2 Para resident in Berlin.

27 Aug 1979 16 Paras killed at Warrenpoint in IRA bomb ambush.

April 1982 Falklands – both 2 and 3 Para win Victoria Crosses in first major action since Second World War.

Nov 1983 5 Infantry Brigade renamed 5 Airborne Brigade.

18 Nov 1989 Mayobridge, Ulster – three Paras of 3rd battalion killed in land mine.

22 June 1990 Prince of Wales, Colonel-in-chief, of the Parachute Regiment heads a parade of 3,500 Paras in London marking Golden Jubilee of Airborne Forces.

August 1990 Elements of 5 Airborne put on standby, after Iraq invades Kuwait.

Sept 1990 Instructors from Parachute Regiment deploy to Gulf on attachment to the American 82nd Airborne.

Oct 1990 Soldiers from 5 Airborne Brigade take part in exercises in Malaysia. The unit remains on Gulf standby, as British Challenger tanks arrive in the region.

HOME FROM THE WAR

ACKNOWLEDGEMENTS
It would have been impossible to assemble the
material for this book without the generous
assistance of many people. In particular we
would like to thank all those from the Parachute
Regiment who helped us at Aldershot and also
the staff of the Airborne Forces Museum.
Thanks are also due to the Imperial War
Museum, Robert Barclay, the Airborne Forces
Museum, the Press Association and Soldier
Magazine who kindly let us use their
photographs and other material.

Designed by Start Studio
Typeset by Central Southern Typesetters,
Eastbourne
Printed in Great Britain by Grosvenor Press
(Portsmouth) Ltd
Based on an idea by Terry Greenwood.
Picture research by Terry Norman and
Terry Greenwood.